HENRY DUNDAS
VISCOUNT MELVILLE

T0382271

Henry Dundas, Viscount Melville

HENRY DUNDAS
VISCOUNT MELVILLE

BY

J. A. LOVAT-FRASER, M.A.

Author of *John Stuart, Earl of Bute*

Cambridge :
at the University Press
1916

CAMBRIDGE
UNIVERSITY PRESS

University Printing House, Cambridge CB2 8BS, United Kingdom

Published in the United States of America by Cambridge University Press, New York

Cambridge University Press is part of the University of Cambridge.

It furthers the University's mission by disseminating knowledge in the pursuit of
education, learning and research at the highest international levels of excellence.

www.cambridge.org
Information on this title: www.cambridge.org/9781107418783

© Cambridge University Press 1916

First published 1916
First paperback edition 2014

A catalogue record for this publication is available from the British Library

ISBN 978-1-107-41878-3 Paperback

CONTENTS

INTRODUCTION

IN St Andrew Square, Edinburgh, the passer-by may
see standing on a lofty pillar the statue of Henry
Dundas, first Viscount Melville, the colleague and friend
of the younger Pitt. The towering height of the monu-
ment is itself emblematic of the lofty position held by
Dundas in his native country at the end of the eighteenth
century. For many years he exercised in Scotland a sway
so absolute that he was nicknamed "Harry the Ninth."
The heaven-soaring statue proclaims to the world how
great was his position in the eyes of his contemporaries.
Beginning as Lord Advocate, he filled in a succession of
British Governments the most important offices, and
played an outstanding part in the history of his time.
No Scottish lawyer has ever attained an influence or
authority equal to that enjoyed by Dundas. In the days
of his greatness, the very streets of Edinburgh, as Sir
Walter Scott said, were thought almost too vulgar for him
to walk upon. His word was law; his will was absolute.
He was "the Pharos of Scotland," said Lord Cockburn.
"Who steered upon him was safe, who disregarded his
light was wrecked. It was to his nod that every man
owed what he had got, and looked for what he wished."

The present writer has been for years an interested
student of the work and career of this remarkable man,
and he has ventured in the following pages to give some

account of his character and surroundings. To tell the complete story of his life is not at present possible, nor is that the object of this sketch. Until the voluminous papers and documents at Melville Castle, the home of Dundas, and at Arniston, in Midlothian, the home of his ancestors, are rendered accessible to research, no biography is possible. In 1887 Mr George Omond published a history of the family of Dundas of Arniston, and stated that, as originally planned, the work included a memoir of its most distinguished member. He added, however, that it was afterwards decided to omit his letters at Arniston, and to make them, with the papers at Melville Castle, the ground-work of a separate biography of Dundas. This has never been done and, until those papers and the numerous other documents at the Record Office and elsewhere are examined or published, it would be idle to attempt a complete account of Dundas's career.

The object of the writer, therefore, in view of what has been said, is, from the materials now available, to delineate a character rather than to unfold a history; to portray a personality rather than to describe a political career. Even in doing so, he is perhaps writing the truest biography. It has been said that Plutarch is the greatest of biographers, because his object was to make a living portrait of a man's inner nature rather than to write the annals of his external acts. "I am not writing *Histories*, but *Lives*," he said. "Very often an action of small note, a short saying, or a jest, shall distinguish a person's real character, more than the greatest sieges, or the most important battles." The aim of the present writer, whether successful or not, is to depict somewhat in the spirit of Plutarch the foremost Scotsman of the eighteenth century. He makes no apology for his work.

Everything is of interest that deals with the marvellous galaxy, which sparkled and flourished in that wonderful time. We read in *The Young Duke* how, when Lord Seymour Temple began a story at White's about Fox and General Fitzpatrick, there was a general retreat, "and the bore," adds the novelist, "as Sir Boyle Roche would say, like the last rose of summer, remains talking to himself." Are there not many of us who would tolerate even bores to-day, if the staple of their talk was stories about Fox and Fitzpatrick and the other statesmen of that brilliant age?

J. A. LOVAT-FRASER.

CHAPTER I

Plutarch quotes a Greek saying that the first requisite to happiness is that a man should be born in a famous city. This requisite to happiness, if it is one, was enjoyed by Henry Dundas, for he was born in the "Bishop's Land," in the High Street of Edinburgh, on 28th April, 1742. The house took its name from having been the town "ludging" of the Archbishops of St Andrews, and bore, above the entry, the legend, "Blessit be ȝe lord for all his giftis, 1578." Dundas was the son of Robert Dundas of Arniston, Lord President of the Court of Session, by his second wife, Anne, daughter of Sir William Gordon of Invergordon. His grandfather, and great-grandfather, as well as his father, had been lords of Session, and he therefore belonged to that *noblesse de robe*, which, in the seventeenth and eighteenth centuries, was as conspicuous a feature of Scottish society as it was of that of France. When Bagehot and other writers call him a "Scotch adventurer," they are unjust, for the house of Arniston was, alike from its legal and political weight, one of the most distinguished and powerful in Scotland, and a member of it might well claim an assured position even among the English Whig magnificoes of the eighteenth century. His eldest brother, nearly thirty years his senior, himself became Lord President, like his father, and continued the tradition of ability and distinction that marked the family.

F. D.   I

After a sound Scottish education at the High School, and University of Edinburgh, Dundas became an advocate on 26th February, 1763. His force and ability soon impressed those who came into contact with him, and his professional progress was as rapid as even the son of one Lord President and the brother of another might expect. There may still be seen, near the head of the Old Fleshmarket Close, the turnpike stair up which his clients climbed to his modest dwelling in his early days. He did not neglect the means that were available for bringing himself to the front. It was the custom at that time of judges and advocates and lairds of position to sit as Elders in the General Assembly of the Church of Scotland, and several of the Scottish politicians, who were afterwards prominent in Parliament, first gave promise of capacity in the business of the Church. Dundas early entered the Assembly, and, as the *Melviad* said,

> " 'Twas in Kirk courts he learned his airs,
> And thunder'd his oration."

He was also active in the Belles Lettres Society, a debating association of young men of education and family, and aired his opinions and views among his equals there. Dr Sommerville, the historian, says that the eminence, which Dundas afterwards attained as a statesman and debater, surpassed the expectations which he had formed from the young advocate's appearances in the two spheres of discussion in which he figured.

Dundas had not to wait long for legal office. In 1766, at the age of twenty-four, he became Solicitor-General for Scotland. In the following year he was one of the counsel for Archibald Douglas of Douglas, the defender in that famous Douglas Cause, which divided Scotland into two bitter and hostile factions. In 1770 his name was included in the list of counsel for the prosecution at the trial of Mungo Campbell for the murder of Alexander, tenth Earl of Eglinton, on the sands near Saltcoats in Ayrshire. As an advocate Dundas was able and at times even brilliant. Alexander Carlyle, minister of Inveresk, said that he entered so warmly into the interest of his client that he totally lost sight of his own personality, and adopted all the feelings, sentiments, and interests, of his client. Carlyle also stated that his method of argument was to make a fair and candid statement of the question under discussion, and then follow it by strong and open reasoning in support of his own. Boswell, himself an advocate, spoke in high praise of Dundas's appearance as counsel in the case of Joseph Knight, the Scottish counterpart of Somersett, who obtained from the English judges the decision that a slave could not breathe in England. "I cannot," says Boswell, "too highly praise the speech which Mr Henry Dundas generously contributed to the cause of the sooty stranger. Mr Dundas's Scottish accent, which has been so often in vain obtruded as an objection to his powerful abilities in Parliament, was no disadvantage to him in his own country. And I do declare that upon this memorable question he impressed me, and I believe all his audience, with such feelings as were produced by some of the most eminent orations of antiquity."

After holding the office of Solicitor-General without a seat in Parliament for eight years, Dundas entered the House of Commons as member for Midlothian in October, 1774, and in May of the following year he became Lord Advocate. In his early life he had been a Whig, and, as an elector of Midlothian, had supported Sir Alexander

Gilmour, who had been an opponent of the Tory administration of Lord Bute. Not long after he entered the
House of Commons he is found figuring as a Parliamentary
reformer. There was a strong desire in Scotland for a
reform of the system of county representation, which,
although supposed to be based on property in land, had
come to have no necessary connexion with either the
possession or the occupation of land. A superior, who
held from the Crown, could create what were merely
fictitious qualifications by splitting and sub-dividing his
holding, and thus outvote the real proprietors. We are
told in *Guy Mannering* how Bertram of Ellangowan and
his factor, Glossin, manufactured voters, and how, "by
dint of clipping and paring here, adding and eking there,
and creating overlords upon all the estate which Bertram
held of the Crown, they advanced at the date of contest,
at the head of ten as good men of parchment as ever took
the oath of trust and possession." An attempt was made
to deal with this abuse, and in October, 1775, Dundas,
at a meeting held in Midlothian, declared himself an
enthusiastic supporter of the proposed legislation. He
hoped, he said, to see the day when the nobleman of
ten thousand pounds a year would not disdain to take off
his hat to the gentlemen of five hundred, and when he
would seek to gain influence, not by a preponderating
number of votes, but by the way in which he did his
duty to his neighbours, and thus deserved popularity.
As a matter of fact, however, in the end nothing came of
the proposal for reform.

Once in the House of Commons, the ability of Dundas
was very quickly recognised, and he was soon regarded
as a coming man. He possessed a strong and masculine
personality; he was bold and courageous, and determined

to make a place for himself in the Parliamentary world.
He never shunned the post of peril; "he went out in
all weathers," as "single-speech" Hamilton said of one
of his contemporaries.

"Pleased with the danger when the waves went high,
He sought the storms."

He was never deterred from defending a measure, of which
he approved, by the violence of opposition or the un-
popularity of the measure itself. His opponents were
never able to daunt him, and were often unable to answer
him. He spoke out, as Sir William Gordon once wrote
to "Jupiter Carlyle," and was afraid of nobody.

When Dundas entered Parliament, the trouble with
the American colonies had already commenced. He long
remained a persistent opponent of conciliation and compromise. His attitude ultimately annoyed the King so
much that in February, 1778, he wrote to his Prime
Minister, Lord North, "The more I think of the conduct
of the Advocate of Scotland the more I am incensed
against him. More favours have been heaped on the
shoulders of that man than ever were bestowed on any
Scotch lawyer, and he seems studiously to embrace an
opportunity to create difficulty. But men of talents,
when not accompanied with integrity, are pests instead
of blessings to society, and true wisdom ought to crush
them rather than nourish them." The contents of the
King's letter were apparently made known to Dundas,
who was keenly alive to the disadvantages attaching to
royal hostility. Soon after this he showed himself more
conciliatory, and the King modified his hostile front.
"Let the Lord Advocate be gained," he wrote in April,
1779, "to attend the whole Session and brave the Parliament, but not for filling employments."

If Dundas was obstinate with regard to the American War, he gave evidence of breadth of mind in another direction. In 1778 he gave notice of a bill to relieve the Scottish Roman Catholics from their disabilities, similar to the English measure introduced by Sir George Savile. An angry agitation, however, was immediately commenced. Petitions were drawn up; protests were signed; and finally riots broke out in Edinburgh, which resulted in the destruction of the Roman Catholic Chapel in Leith Wynd, and in other acts of violence. A crazy nobleman, Lord George Gordon, himself the descendant of a historic house, which had suffered much for its loyalty to the Catholic Faith, placed himself at the head of the "No Popery" agitation, and concluded his services to Protestantism by bringing about the famous London riots, which have been so graphically described by Dickens in *Barnaby Rudge*. In the end the opposition to the repeal bill proved so formidable that Dundas had to abandon it.

In 1781 an event took place, which had an important influence on the life of Dundas. The younger Pitt took his seat in Parliament at the age of twenty-one. The condition of Great Britain at the time was deplorable in the extreme. She was engaged in hostilities with France, Spain, Holland, and the American colonies, and was overwhelmed with debt. Lord North was opposed by two sections of Whigs, the followers of Lord Rockingham, who enjoyed the support of distinguished *novi homines* like Burke and Sheridan, and the followers of Lord Shelburne, whose bond of union was their former adherence to Pitt's father, Lord Chatham. Pitt naturally joined the party of Lord Shelburne, and attacked the contest with America in the strongest terms. It was, he said, "a most accursed, wicked, barbarous, cruel, unnatural, unjust, and diabolical war." From the very first Dundas, with keen discernment, seems to have concluded that Pitt was the man of the future. He had to oppose Pitt's attacks on the war, but he took care at the same time to pave the way to a rapprochement with his youthful opponent. There is the climbing genus in man as well as in plants, says Hazlitt, and Dundas was of the sort of men, who are destined to rise. As a Scot, he had obstacles to overcome in the governing circles of England, which an Englishman would have escaped, and he intuitively realised that, in union with Pitt, his ambitions would be most easily realised. He determined to act in the spirit of Pope's lines,

> "Be thou the first true merit to befriend,
> His praise is lost, who stays till all commend."

He was careful, while opposing Pitt, to lavish encomiums on the happy union of "first-rate abilities, high integrity, bold and honest independence of conduct, and the most persuasive eloquence," that were combined in the young member. This attitude he never ceased to maintain, until Pitt and he became political allies.

On 20th March, 1782, the unhappy ministry of Lord North succumbed to the forces ranged against it. In a series of letters, written to John Robinson, the under-secretary of the Treasury, just before the retreat of his chief, Dundas protested his affection for North, and his determination to stand and fall with him. "I feel it," he wrote, "as a point of private honour in my own breast, which I value more than any situation, to stop my political career with the fall of the minister, whose friend I have been." It is not necessary to attach too much importance to those protestations, which were intended partly, no doubt, for the consumption of North. Dundas was never

a man to make an unnecessary enemy, or to needlessly
alienate a friend. Walter Scott, in his brilliant sketch of
Queen Caroline in the *Heart of Midlothian*, says that it
was one of her maxims to bear herself towards her political
friends with such caution, as if there was a possibility of
their one day being her enemies, and towards political
opponents with the same degree of circumspection as if
they might again become friendly to her measures. This
maxim, dating from the *Ajax* of Sophocles, was also that
of Dundas, and in leaving North he wished to leave him
with feelings of friendship and goodwill that might be
useful in the future.

When Lord North resigned the premiership, his
place was taken by Lord Rockingham. Fox became
Foreign Secretary, and Shelburne Home and Colonial
Secretary, while Dundas continued to hold his office of
Lord Advocate. In the new administration Dundas's
attention was chiefly concerned with Indian affairs. In
April of the previous year a committee had been appointed
to report on the causes of the war in the Carnatic, and the
state of the British possessions in that part of India, and
Dundas had been appointed chairman. Great dissatisfaction existed with regard to British administration in
the East, and Dundas saw that his appointment as chairman of the enquiry would give him an opportunity of
acquiring *kudos* and reputation. In April, 1782, the
committee brought in six reports, and on the 9th of the
month Dundas addressed the House of Commons in
committee on the causes and extent of the troubles in
the East. He accused the Presidencies of plundering
and oppression, and moved a number of resolutions,
reflecting severely on the administration of the East
India Company, and particularly on Sir Thomas Rumbold,

Governor of Madras.   Rumbold is said to have commenced
life as a waiter in White's[1], and had, by dubious methods,
acquired vast wealth as a ruler in India.   The resolutions
of Dundas were carried, but he could never induce the
House of Commons to take effectual action against the
culprits.   Rumbold and his associates had powerful
friends, and they were never brought to book.   A resolution was passed calling on the East India Company to
recall Warren Hastings, but this was never done, and he
remained in India till 1785.

The administration of Rockingham was far from being
a tranquil one.   Negotiations for peace with America were
entered upon and proved no easy task.   Rockingham was
feeble and indecisive.   Fox and Shelburne were jealous
and at variance with one another.   Dundas, amid the
strife and troubles, kept his eye on the future, and continued to eulogise Pitt, even when he opposed him.   He
was, at the same time, so uncivil to his colleague, Fox,
that the latter said that either he or Dundas must resign
and was only placated by Dundas's assurance of good
will.   The administration continued to be a tempestuous
one, however, until its final collapse with the death of
Rockingham on 1st July, 1782.

Lord Rockingham was succeeded by Lord Shelburne.
The new premier was a man of great ability, courage, and
political knowledge, a master of finance, experienced in
affairs, and no mean orator.   But he was cursed by a
reputation for insincerity and duplicity, which obtained
for him the nickname of *Malagrida*[2], and led the King
to describe him as the "Jesuit of Berkeley Square."
Pitt became Chancellor of the Exchequer in the new

---

[1] He is probably the original of Lord Fitzwarene in *Sybil*.
[2] A notorious Jesuit.

administration. Fox had endeavoured on the death of
Rockingham to impose another aristocratic figurehead
on the King in the person of the Duke of Portland, and
so to continue the domination of "the great Revolution
families." Failing in this endeavour, he refused to take
office under Shelburne. Shelburne justified his stand
against Fox by citing the authority of Chatham, who, he
said, always declared that the country ought not to be
governed by any oligarchical party or family connexion,
and that, if it was to be so governed, the Constitution
must of necessity expire[1]. Shelburne showed his sense
of the value of Dundas's services by not only retaining
him as Lord Advocate, but by also admitting him to the
Privy Council, appointing him Treasurer of the Navy
and Keeper of the Scottish Signet for life, and giving him
"the recommendation of all offices which should fall
vacant in Scotland." This grant of the patronage of
his native country was the foundation on which Dundas
subsequently built up the great power and influence in
Scotland, which earned for him the nickname of "Harry
the Ninth."

The ministry of Shelburne brought the American War
to a final conclusion by the treaty of Versailles, but it did
little more. Fox, irritated and chagrined by Shelburne's
attainment of office, joined forces with his former enemy,
North, and thereby filled the world with astonishment
and disgust. Gibbon, when at Lausanne, told a friend
that Dundas almost went upon his knees to dissuade
North from this ruinous alliance. The character of Fox
was indelibly stained by his action. He had been the
unsparing assailant of his new ally, and had charged him

[1] This was not always Chatham's view. Vide *John Stuart,
Earl of Bute*, by the present writer, page 63.

over and over again with corruption, incapacity, treachery, and falsehood. He had pronounced him void of honour and honesty, and in March, 1782, had declared in Parliament that he would rest satisfied to be called "the most infamous of mankind," could he for a moment think of making terms with such a man. And now the nation saw with amazement the flagrant union of Fox with the object of his envenomed scurrility. The scandal was rendered complete, when Fox, who had denounced the American War for years, joined with North, who had carried it on, in opposing and censuring the treaty of Peace.

CHAPTER II

The uneasy reign of Shelburne was brought to an end by a defeat in the House of Commons on 22nd February, 1783, and two days afterwards the Prime Minister resigned. In doing so he advised the King to send for Pitt. Dundas claimed credit for urging his chief to take this step, and on the 25th he spoke of the plan as "my project," but, as Dr Holland Rose has pointed out, Dundas did not originate the idea. The King eagerly adopted the suggestion of Shelburne, and Dundas pressed Pitt with urgency to take advantage of the invitation. For a few hours Pitt appeared to be disposed to consent, but eventually, with a prudence and foresight singular in so young a man, he refused the tempting bait. The excitement felt by Dundas, while the matter lay in the balance, is reflected in the letters which he wrote in rapid succession to his brother, the Lord President, in Edinburgh and which are given in Lord Stanhope's biography of Pitt.

The refusal of Pitt compelled the King, very much against his will, to send for the Duke of Portland. In the new administration Fox and North were joint Secretaries of State. If the public indignation at the political alliance of those two politicians was great, it was vastly increased when they became members of the same ministry. Walpole speaks of the "cartloads" of abusive and satiric prints, which were current at the time. The dull Duke of

Portland was jeered at as "a fit block to hang Whigs on," and George Selwyn said that the Duke's elevation reminded him of the old Puritan tract, *A Shove to an Heavy-breached Christian*. Dundas was retained in his office of Lord Advocate, but his post of Treasurer of the Navy was given to Charles Townshend. In April, 1783, Dundas brought in a bill to make certain improvements in the administration of India. He proposed to send out a new Governor-General with power to overrule, if he thought it needful, the wish and the opinion of the Council. He indicated Lord Cornwallis as the fittest person to govern India, and, in doing so, pointed out in his speech one of the principal evils of Eastern administration. "Here," he said, "there was no broken fortune to be mended! Here was no avarice to be gratified! Here was no beggarly mushroom kindred to be provided for! no crew of hungry followers, gaping to be gorged!" Dundas did not receive any encouragement from the ministry, and his attempt came to nothing.

In August, 1783, Dundas was removed from his office of Lord Advocate at the instance of Fox, and replaced by Henry Erskine. There had been continual friction between the two, and Dundas had taken up a high and mighty line that had irritated his colleagues. "It began to be seriously credited," wrote Lord Loughborough to Fox, "that it was not permitted to them (the administration) to remove any person (in Scotland) protected by Dundas." To eradicate this impression Fox had the boaster dismissed. It is said that shortly after the event, Erskine, the new Lord Advocate, casually met his predecessor in the Parliament House in Edinburgh, and playfully remarked that he was about to order the silk gown that was the official costume of the Lord Advocate. "It is

hardly worth while for the time you will want it," said
Dundas, "you had better borrow mine." "Thank you,"
said Erskine, "but it never shall be said of Henry Erskine
that he adopted the abandoned habits of his predecessor."

The affairs of India were now calling so urgently for
attention that Fox introduced another measure for the
reform of the government. He proposed in his bill to
give the whole patronage of India and the entire control
of the government to an irresponsible board of seven
persons, all charters or vested rights notwithstanding.
Those seven persons were to hold office for four years
from the passing of the Act, whatever changes of administration might ensue in Great Britain. Amongst the
provisions of the bill, this proposal was the one which
instantly seized the attention of the Opposition, and
excited the strongest hostility. "It is, I really think,"
wrote Pitt, "the boldest and most unconstitutional
measure ever attempted, transferring at one stroke, in
spite of all charters and compacts, the immense patronage
and influence of the East to Charles Fox, in or out of
office." North himself described it as a good receipt to
knock up an administration. The bill, supported by the
eloquence of Fox and Burke, passed the House of Commons,
but when it came to the House of Lords, the King communicated to Lord Temple a statement that he should
regard any peer, who voted for it, not only as not a friend,
but as an enemy. The personal intervention of the King
proved fatal to the measure, and on the 17th December
the bill was rejected by the peers. On the same night
Fox vented a tirade against the King, in which he in-
directly drew a parallel between George and Tiberius.
He likened the written communication to Lord Temple to
the perfidious rescript sent by Tiberius to the Roman

Senate, in which he incited that body to despatch Sejanus
without a trial, and without evidence of his guilt.   On the
night after that speech the King sent to Fox and North
a message ordering them to surrender the seals.   Fox was
amazed.   "He would not dare do it," he exclaimed.
He had evidently yet to learn that there were many
bold things the King would do in the exercise of what
he believed to be his duty.

On the fall of the Portland ministry, the King immediately turned to Pitt, who accepted office without the
slightest hesitation.   His action excited the ridicule and
satire of the dismissed ministers, who still commanded a
majority in the House of Commons.   When the writ for
Pitt's re-election was moved, there was loud and general
laughter among Fox and his allies, who professed to treat
the whole thing as a subject for gibe and jest.   It was said
that Pitt's government was a mince-pie administration,
which would end with the Christmas holidays.   And at first
it looked as if it might be so, for Pitt found great difficulty
in filling the offices.   Eventually he got together a cabinet,
which consisted of himself and six peers.   It was upon
Dundas, who again became Treasurer of the Navy, that
Pitt relied as his chief assistant in debate.   Pitt's debt
to the Scottish lawyer in the earlier days of their association was very great.   Not only was Pitt inexperienced
and ignorant of mankind, but he had a cold and un-
attractive manner, which repelled those around him.
Lytton's line about Lord John Russell in the *New Timon*
might have been applied to the new premier,

"He wants your votes, but your affection not."

Dundas had nothing of the moral grandeur, the disinterestedness, or the eloquence of Pitt, but the latter
would never have done what he did, but for Dundas's

knowledge of human nature, his acute political judgment, his skill in handling men, his experience in political strategy, his acquaintance with business, his popular and conciliatory manners.

The task that now lay before Pitt was an appalling one. The finances were in great disorder. Foreign affairs, and especially the commercial relations with the new American republic required immediate attention. The administration of India called for speedy reform. Pitt was fronted by an angry Opposition, which included giants like Fox and Burke and Sheridan, and which was stung to the quick by the preferment of a mere boy. The janissaries of the Whig leaders vilified and railed at Pitt with malignant persistence, and defeated him again and again in a series of contemptible victories. Fox refused the least respite to the administration, and even attacked the Sovereign through his young Minister, making it, as Samuel Johnson afterwards said, a contest whether the nation should be ruled by the sceptre of George the Third or by the tongue of Fox. Nothing, however, shook the tenacity of Pitt. Side by side through it all, Dundas and his chief fought with unabated resolution, and no mediaeval knight was ever more gallantly served by his squire than the youthful premier by his Scottish henchman.

The hostility and factious conduct of the Opposition not only did not shake Pitt; it aroused sympathy with him in the world outside. The nation, watching the contest with eager interest, was no less filled with admiration of the Prime Minister than it was disgusted by the violence of his opponents. Hazlitt said that Fox had too much of the milk of human kindness to be a practical statesman, and that he was "too generous an enemy." It was just his want of the milk of human kindness and of generosity that alienated the world now, and strengthened the hands of his opponent. The King and those around Pitt, observing his increasing popularity, urged him to appeal to the electorate, but the minister saw that the time was not yet ripe. Soon the nation began to move. The Corporation of London thanked the King for dismissing his Ministers, and other towns and public bodies followed suit. The rank and file in the House of Commons began to waver in its support of Fox. The final struggle came on 8th March, 1784, when a debate took place on the King's refusal to accede to a request, which had been made to him by the Opposition majority, to remove his Ministers. Pitt took little part in the discussion, and Dundas was the hero of the night. "Seldom," said Wraxall, "have I heard Dundas, during the course of his long and brilliant career, display more ability or eloquence than on that evening." Fox only carried his motion by 191 to 190, and at last it was clear that the game was up. Pitt appealed to the country, and at the ensuing general election the members of the Opposition were smitten hip and thigh. Pitt resumed the government of the Empire, and attacked the difficult problems of statesmanship that awaited solution with the support of a loyal and substantial majority.

Pitt's first measure was to restore order to the national finances. The opinions and sympathies of Pitt were essentially those of the great mercantile class, whose good opinion he sedulously cultivated. He found congenial employment in the manipulation of finance, and the development of industry and commerce. He was what Grattan called him in another connexion, an "inspired accountant." He realised the increasing importance which trade questions were assuming in English politics, and in 1786 he reconstructed the Board of Trade, which became one of the most efficient departments of the administration. He brought to his duties, as trustee of the public purse, a punctilious solicitude for the public interest, and a rigorous accuracy in managing the national finance that worked like magic. He recognised the truth of Burke's words, that public frugality is national strength. He reduced and equalised duties and diffused them over a wide area. He instituted the consolidated fund, which, by combining scores of small accounts into one large account, simplified administration and promoted economy. His financial statements were masterpieces of comprehensive and lucid exposition. Mr Gladstone, in one of his own financial speeches, cited Mallet du Pan's description of Pitt's Budget speech of 1798. "It is not a speech spoken by the minister," said Mallet du Pan, "it is a complete course of public economy; a work, and one of the finest works upon practical and theoretical finance that ever distinguished the pen of a philosopher and statesman."

After restoring the finances Pitt dealt with the administration of India, and established the dual system of government by the Crown and the East India Company, which lasted with some modifications till 1858. The directors of the Company were to exercise their functions under the superintendence of a Board of Control, presided over by a President, who, as a member of the ministry, was to be responsible to Parliament. Patronage was to be retained by the directors, but the Governor-General and the more important officers were to be chosen subject to the pleasure of the Crown, and were to be liable to be dismissed by the Crown. Dundas was appointed a member of the Board of Control on 3rd September, 1784, and, although Pitt himself attended the Board regularly and thoroughly mastered its business, Dundas was the dominant power from the first.

It is interesting to find that, a few weeks after the establishment of the Board, Lord Sydney wrote complaining of the undue number of Scotsmen, who were receiving appointments   There is no doubt that, from his first connexion with the Board, Dundas adopted a policy, steadily pursued, of sending out young Scotsmen to the Eastern Empire.   During the eighteenth century the status and position of the Scottish aristocracy had been changed for the worse.   They had lost much of their power with the Union in 1707.   Many of them had suffered in the Jacobite Risings of 1715 and 1745, and had forfeited their estates.   The abolition of heritable jurisdictions had been a severe blow to their prestige.   Stript of their power, they had no wealth to compensate for its loss. Agriculture was in its infancy, and mercantile pursuits were, for the most part, despised as beneath their dignity. The consequence was that Scotland was full of young men of good birth, hardy and ambitious, possessed of the ability and self-reliance of their nation, "the lofty Scot" as Thomson says,

> "To hardship tamed, active in arts and arms,
> Fir'd with a restless, an impatient flame,
> That leads him raptur'd where ambition calls."

It was from this class that Dundas recruited the Indian service.   He knew the qualities of his countrymen and recognised that he was safe in placing them in positions of responsibility.   As Burton says of the Scottish soldiers of fortune of a century before, they had those habits of command, that unlearnable self-estimate, which insensibly

2—2

exacts obedience.   In sending Scots to the East Dundas
strengthened his influence in India by filling the administration with capable men, devoted to his interest, and
strengthened his influence in Scotland, where gratitude
for favours, past and to come, kept the people loyal to
his standard.   As Lord Rosebery has put it, he Scotticised
India, and Orientalised Scotland.   The second Earl of
Minto told Lord Stanhope, the historian, that there was
scarcely a gentleman's family in Scotland, of whatever
politics, that had not at some time received some Indian
appointment or some act of kindness from Dundas.   In
1821, years after the death of Dundas, Walter Scott
described the Board of Control as "the Corn Chest for
Scotland, where we poor gentry must send our younger
sons, as we send our black cattle to the South."

The process of Scotticising India was not, however,
suffered to go on without complaints from Englishmen.
Protests are found from time to time in the political
correspondence of the period.   The lampooners could not
overlook so promising a subject for satire.   Gillray's
cartoon in March, 1787, *The Board of Control or the
Blessings of a Scotch Dictator*, expresses contemporary
feeling.   It represents a table with three people sitting
at it, one of whom is Dundas, who is placed at the end,
while the other two, who are Pitt and Lord Sydney, the
President of the Board, are playing at the childish game
of push-pin.   Four ragged Scotsmen in short kilts are
standing beside Dundas, who has a number of documents
before him.   One of them is a petition from the Bakers'
Company saying that so many "raw young Scotchmen"
had been sent to India that journeymen bakers could not
be procured, and asking "your mightiness" to appoint
some Englishmen.   Another document is a list of "fit

persons to succeed in the Direction," which includes such names as Fraser, Stuart, McLeod, McPherson, McLean and McDonald.

In August, 1784, Dundas acquired great popularity in Scotland by bringing in a measure to restore the estates, which had been forfeited after the Jacobite Rising of 1745, to the rightful heirs. The recipients of the estates were to compensate the government for sums expended on improvements, and on liquidating encumbrances, and those sums were to be devoted chiefly to the completion of the canal between the Forth and the Clyde—a work of national importance. In introducing the measure Dundas gratified Pitt by quoting the famous speech of his father, Lord Chatham, in which he had praised the Highlanders, and had said that, disdaining to enquire whether a man had been rocked in a cradle to the North, or to the South, of the Tweed, he had sought for merit, where he could discover it. In introducing this measure, which was easily passed, Dundas had partly in view the stemming of the tide of emigration which was rapidly depopulating the Highlands. Thousands were leaving Scotland for America, as the result of the breakdown of clanship and the disappearance of the ancient chiefs. Dundas hoped to bring back, by restoring the estates, the beneficent sway of the old landlord chief. His hope, alas! was a vain one, and the tide of emigration continued to flow.

The future was now looking rosy for Dundas, and his worldly wisdom in attaching himself to Pitt was manifest to all. Wraxall speaks with wonder of the position which he had acquired at the end of the session in August, 1784. "Only nine months earlier," says Wraxall, "he presented the melancholy spectacle of a Scotch advocate proscribed by the coalition, without apparent chance of public employment, nearly destitute of fortune, and unprovided with official means of subsistence." Now he had gained the second place in the administration, and had made himself indispensable to his chief. Sitting on the Treasury bench in the House of Commons, he came into continual contact with Pitt, defended him when personally attacked, and, after the House rose, frequently accompanied him home to Downing Street. The Opposition, jealous of his increasing power, affected to treat him as a venal deserter, who had only attached himself to Pitt from motives of calculating ambition, and made him the butt of their satires and lampoons. "But," says Wraxall, "they found his hide impenetrable, fenced with good humour, protected by great abilities, strength of character, and corresponding manliness of mind."

CHAPTER III

At this point in the narrative it may be useful to say something about the character of Pitt, with whose fortunes those of Dundas were so closely entwined. That character is still to a large extent shrouded in obscurity. "Frankly, what do we know about Pitt?" asks Mr Fortescue[1]. "I cannot help thinking that we know remarkably, I might almost say, disgracefully little." There are endless questions about his character and life that still remain without an answer. The main outlines of his career are patent enough. He became Prime Minister as a youth of twenty-four, in face of a powerful and bitterly hostile opposition. He had for a long time no colleagues who were of any value in debate, with the exception of Dundas. Yet in spite of many disadvantages, he not only held his own in Parliament at the beginning of his ministry, but he attacked in succession every difficult problem of statesmanship that awaited solution. He rescued Great Britain from the degradation into which corruption and incompetence had plunged her. He set an example of pure and self-denying patriotism, which raised the level of public life, and introduced a new standard of public feeling. By his unwearying exertions, his enlightened views in regard to commerce and finance, and his ready invention of resources, he reorganised the

[1] *British Statesmen of the Great War.*

finances of the kingdom, he replenished the exchequer, and he brought the trade and commerce of the country into a state of unprecedented prosperity. In India, as at home, he proved a constructive statesman. He would have given the wisest relief to Ireland, if he had not been prevented by a factious opposition. He made a treaty of commerce with France that proved eminently beneficial to British trade. He endeavoured, though unsuccessfully, to deal with Parliamentary reform. In 1782, in 1783, and in 1788, he brought the matter before the House of Commons, and on the last two occasions with the support of Dundas, and it was not his fault that the House rejected his proposals. His greatness is to be measured not merely by his individual genius, but by the circumstances in which he worked, and the difficulties which he had to face and overcome. He was the man on whom, through long years of peril, the nation relied with absolute confidence, and whose death was regarded as an irreparable calamity. Cowper had once uttered the despairing cry about his country,

"Once Chatham saved thee, but who saves thee now?"

Pitt, no less than his father, was the preserver of his country.

One of the secrets of Pitt's success was the inexorable firmness and consistency with which he asserted and maintained his own political supremacy. He had an austere and lofty dignity and self-reliance, which repelled all possibility of a liberty or of undue familiarity, and which compelled his colleagues into an attitude of deference. Much of the disunion and rivalry in previous administrations had been due to the want of a strong head, who could compel obedience and deference. Dundas himself, for example, said of Lord North, that he wanted only

one quality to render him a great and distinguished statesman, namely a more despotic and commanding temper.
Pitt, as long as he was chief minister, was always master
at the Council table. The Duke of Newcastle said of
Pitt's father, when they were colleagues in the same
cabinet, that the whole council dreaded his frown.
Chatham's son dominated his cabinets perhaps not by
the same methods as his father, but quite as effectively.
From the very beginning of Pitt's ministry, Dundas, the
old experienced "Parliamentary hand," fell in behind the
youthful Prime Minister without a thought of rivalry, and
acknowledged without question the supremacy of Pitt's
abilities and character. Lord Stanhope, speaking of his
examination of the correspondence at Melville Castle, says
that the letters of Pitt to Dundas before the latter was
raised to the peerage, begin "Dear Dundas," while Dundas
always writes to his leader as "My dear Sir." There is·
a world of meaning under this difference in the mode of
address.

Pitt had boundless self-confidence, and never shrank
from taking responsibility. He possessed dauntless
courage and constancy and was never crushed by misfortunes. He possessed an invincible hopefulness and
optimism. It is said *magni est animi semper sperare*, but
there are those who think that his confidence and hopefulness were carried too far, and led him into blunders that
might have been avoided. Dr Holland Rose says that
his optimism was his besetting sin. His personal disinterestedness was unique in his day. Neither ambition
nor interest ever jostled him out of the straight path of
duty or even made him flag or languish in his course. He
had a nice and jealous honour, in comparison with which
everything else was dust and ashes. He had in his gift

stars and garters, lucrative offices, honours and dignities, and he remained himself poor and untitled. He might have used the words which Quintus Curtius puts into the mouths of the soldiers of Alexander, *Omnium victores, omnium inopes sumus.* The style of his oratory was in keeping with his personal characteristics, strong, copious, and dignified, with few purple patches,

> "And even reluctant party feels a while
> The gracious power: as thro' the varied maze
> Of eloquence, now smooth, now quick, now strong,
> Profound and clear, you roll the copious flood[1]."

Pitt had an extraordinary power of assimilating knowledge, yet he was hardly ever seen with a book in his hand, after he became minister, and Dean Pellew suggests that he must have extracted information from those he conversed with, as plants imbibe nutriment from the air around them. He freely relied upon his followers for the ideas and theories, which his influence and eloquence translated into practice. No great minister, as the Dropmore Papers show, more often appropriated the ideas of others, or was more readily guided by the advice of able colleagues. It may be doubted whether he was ordinarily a hard worker. "You know," said Wilberforce, "how difficult, I may say, next to impossible it is, to extract a line from Pitt." His long silences and his failure to give the decision that was urgently required were defects in his fine character, and had serious consequences on repeated occasions. The mantle of isolation, with which he clothed himself, was a great disadvantage in the conduct of business, but it clung to him through life. "Pitt does not make friends," wrote Wilberforce in 1785. Lord

[1] Thomson, in his description of Chesterfield's oratory in *The Seasons, Winter.*

Holland relates that he knew few even of his own relations till he became immersed in politics. He knew nothing of his first cousins, the Grenvilles, with whom he was afterwards so closely associated, till they came into Parliament. "Thomas Grenville," says Lord Holland, "told me (what seems incredible) that he never was in his company till 1793; and Lord Erskine assured me that in Alice's Coffee-house, when William Grenville (afterwards Lord Grenville) came in, Mr Pitt, who was drinking tea with Erskine, asked who that young man was."

Between this austere and lofty minister and his Scottish subordinate, there grew up an intimate friendship of the closest description. It gradually increased in strength, until it became one of the remarkable features of the political life of the time, and the duumvirate, as the two colleagues were nicknamed, were bound together by a mutual confidence that was perfect. When Dundas was appointed Home Secretary in 1791, he had become Pitt's closest friend and most trusted colleague. "Mr Pitt," wrote Dundas, "among the multitude of things, which press upon him, is at all times ready to accommodate himself to my call." In 1794 the Prime Minister wrote of every act of Dundas "being as much mine as his." Dundas was the companion with whom Pitt passed his convivial hours. In the words of Cicero, he was, to his chief, *magno adjumento in periculis, solacio in laboribus, gratulationi in victoria*. Dundas possessed a villa at Wimbledon, to which he was accustomed to repair after debates, for the purpose of sleeping in the fresh air of the country. Pitt, on quitting the Treasury bench, used to throw himself into Dundas's post-chaise, and to go to Wimbledon with him. At whatever hour they arrived, they sat down to supper, and never failed to drink each his bottle. Even

in the familiar intercourse of what might be termed his
leisure, Pitt spent much of the time on the discussion of
business. He was different from Fox, who, according to
Sir James Mackintosh, disliked political conversation, and
never willingly took part in it. After Pitt's death Dundas
wrote to Lord Lowther that he did not recollect, during
the many years in which Pitt and he had lived in close
association, that they ever had a walk or a ride together,
without a very considerable part of the time being occupied
in discussions relating to public affairs.

A comparison instituted between the two ministers by
Wraxall helps to explain the success of their close and
intimate union

"Nor could Pitt," says Wraxall, "have discovered a more
able, efficient, laborious, and eloquent coadjutor than Dundas,
if he had sought throughout his majesty's dominions. That
he wanted the correct and measured deportment, the elevated
disinterestedness, and the insensibility or superiority to female
seductions, by which qualities the first minister was distinguished, we must admit; but he possessed, on the other hand,
many endowments of mind or of disposition, vainly sought in
the Chancellor of the Exchequer. Dundas manifested more
amenity of manner, more placability of temper, more facility of
access, a more yielding, accommodating, and forgiving manner.
If Pitt subdued, Dundas conciliated, adversaries. The latter,
who had received his political education, and imbibed his
parliamentary habits, under Lord North, breathed a more
liberal spirit, more comprehensive in its embrace, and more
calculated to gain or to disarm his opponents. Pitt was
undoubtedly capable of firm and fervent friendships; yet
Dundas, with less sincerity, acquired more general good will.
Pitt was cold and repulsive; Dundas invited approach. The
former seldom made advances, mingled a gravity or a con-
straint even with his civilities, seemed to weigh his expressions,
rarely provoked or prolonged conversations, and speedily
retired into himself. The latter was always communicative,
and the lineaments of his countenance, open, as well as gay,

facilitated his objects even when he most concealed his purposes. Pitt appeared as if made to withhold, Dundas to
confer, ministerial favours.''

Wraxall states that Dundas kept a jealous eye on any
one that was likely to prove a rival in the confidence of
his chief. He mentions a piece of gossip that shows, if
it is true, how vigilant Pitt's henchman was in guarding
his influence. His story is that at one time the Duchess
of Gordon, who was very intimate with both Pitt and
Dundas, formed the design of marrying her daughter,
Lady Charlotte, to Pitt. Pitt, although indifferent to
women as a rule, had manifested some partiality for her,
and had shown her some attention. The Duchess desirous
of improving such promising appearances, used to drive
to Wimbledon with her daughter at times when she knew
that Pitt was there. But the jealousy of · Dundas was
speedily aroused, and he counteracted her design in a
curious but efficacious way. He had divorced his first
wife, and was free to marry again. He affected a desire
to lay his own person and fortunes at the feet of Lady
Charlotte. Pitt, who had never displayed more than a
slight inclination, ceased his attentions, and Dundas,
having thus separated his chief and the lady, himself
abandoned his pretensions and retired from the field.
One's sympathy rather goes out to Lady Charlotte, and
it is satisfactory to learn that two years later she married
Colonel Charles Lennox who became fourth Duke of
Richmond.

When it is suggested that Dundas was unscrupulous
and self-seeking, the best warning against accepting that
view too implicitly is the fact that a statesman of Pitt's
high moral character made a close friend of him for so
many years. The political world is like a net that brings

up good fish and bad, and men of high character have often to associate and work with men who are the reverse. But they do not become their intimate friends and constant associates. It is a truism that a man is known by the company he keeps. *Noscitur a sociis.* Wilberforce thought that Dundas's influence had injured the purer character of Pitt. "His connexion with Dundas was Pitt's great misfortune," said Wilberforce, for he adds, "Dundas was a loose man." Yet Wilberforce himself in the same passage goes on to modify the severity of his judgment on Dundas. "People have thought him a mean, intriguing creature," he says, "but he was in many respects a fine warm-hearted fellow." Dundas did not stand on the moral level of Pitt, but his level was at all events high enough to make it possible for Pitt and himself to be the Orestes and Pylades of politics for many a year.

CHAPTER IV

In 1786 the affairs of India again came before the House of Commons. In March Dundas brought in a bill to empower the Governor-General of India to give the ultimate decision in all measures of administration, whether the supreme council agreed with him or not. This action called forth the exaggerated and loud-voiced opposition of Burke. He denounced it as a libel on the liberties and constitution of England and an attempt to establish a Turkish tyranny throughout the British dominions in the East. It was, he stated, "a raw-head and bloody bones, a new Star Chamber, subverting Magna Charta." The excited orator went on, "When Hypocrisy has finished her game, and Profligacy comes in turn to act her part,

'Then shall the warlike Harry, like himself,
Assume the port of Mars, and at his heels,
Leash'd in like hounds, shall Famine, Fire, and Sword,
Crouch for employment.'"

The quotation from Shakespeare was a happy one, for Dundas was always known among his friends as "Harry." Dundas dismissed Burke's outburst as the mere flight of a wild and disordered imagination, and in the end the Bill passed without difficulty.

At this stage it will be well to deal with a matter at once interesting and obscure, the conduct of Dundas towards Warren Hastings. In 1785 Hastings, after a

long and distinguished career in India, returned to
England.   His services to the Empire procured for
him a most favourable reception.   The directors of the
East India Company greeted him with a public address,
and the King and Queen were most gracious to him.
That Hastings deserved to be honoured is beyond all
question.   He may have been a severe and autocratic
ruler, but it must be remembered that he belonged to
a small garrison set down in a vast and hostile country,
and that severity was the best weapon to safeguard his
position.   Weakness inevitably meant disaster and death.
Favourably as Hastings had been received, however, he
had two determined enemies in Parliament in Burke and
Philip Francis, who were resolved, if they could, to bring
him to the dust.   The first attack was made by Burke,
who impugned the conduct of Hastings in the Rohilla
war.   Dundas had, in 1782, condemned the attack on
the Rohillas, and the Opposition, believing that Dundas
was going to support Hastings, hoped to "corner" him
by bringing up his own former condemnation.   But
Dundas was "an old Parliamentary hand," and was
ready to defend his change of front.   He said that he
still thought the attack on the Rohillas unjust, but that
in the former vote of censure he and his friends had only
aimed at the recall and not the penal prosecution of
Hastings.   Not only had they not brought about the
recall, but an Act of Parliament had subsequently
appointed Hastings Governor-General of Bengal.   After
that Act, which might be regarded as a Parliamentary
pardon, said Dundas, Hastings had rendered services so
great that they might almost be tempted to call him the
saviour of India.   Pitt voted with Dundas, and Burke
was defeated by 119 to 67.

The next charge was brought by Fox, and dealt with Chait Singh, Raja of Benares, on whom an enormous fine had been imposed by Hastings. To the amazement of all, Pitt supported Fox. He said that to levy a fine of £500,000, as had been done, for delay in paying a contribution of £50,000, which had been paid after all, was to destroy all connexion between the degrees of guilt and punishment, and was repugnant to reason and justice. Dundas took no part in the debate, but voted with Fox, who carried his resolution by 119 to 79. Pitt's action in voting on the second charge with those who were attacking Hastings has been severely, but quite unjustly, condemned. It has been said that Pitt and Dundas were jealous of Hastings, and feared his advent to the Board of Control or Parliament. Wraxall and Bland Burges asserted that Dundas had somehow become convinced that the King intended to remove him from the Board of Control, and put Hastings in his place. Dundas, according to Bland Burges, sedulously fanned Pitt's jealousy and uneasiness and so alarmed his mind that he hurried him on to a decision before he had time to satisfy himself as to its justice or expediency. Hastings himself, who hated Dundas, also in later life ascribed Pitt's abandonment of him to the same unworthy influence. Some thirty years later he told a story that on the morning of 13th June Dundas called on Pitt, remained closeted with him for some hours, and convinced him that he must vote against the ex-viceroy.

Dr Holland Rose, who goes carefully into the charges against Pitt in this connexion, wholly rejects the theory that Pitt was influenced by the jealousy of Dundas. He says that from the beginning of the Hastings case Pitt had sought to hold the balances even, and had left it open to his colleagues to differ from him. He quotes a letter of Wilberforce which points to a sincere desire to get at the truth about the case. "He paid as much impartial attention to it," said Wilberforce, "as if he were a juryman." There is no good reason to doubt that Pitt's decision was the result of honest conviction, and that Dundas was right, when he wrote to Lord Cornwallis, "The truth is, when we examined the various articles of charges against him (Hastings), with his defences, they were so strong, and the defences so perfectly unsupported, it was impossible not to concur."

The third charge against Hastings, which related to the Begams of Oudh, was brought forward by Sheridan in a speech of remarkable eloquence. Pitt again supported the motion, and it was duly carried. Eventually it was decided to impeach Hastings, and Burke was given the first place among the managers. Burke wished to include Philip Francis, but the rancorous hostility, always shown by Francis towards Hastings, made the proposal repugnant to the House. Dundas supported Burke's motion, but Pitt opposed it, and Francis was rejected. Dundas was unable to conceal his pleasure at the impeachment, according to Burges, who tells a story about him which may mean anything or nothing. Lord Maitland, one of the managers, asked Dundas in presence of Burges, his opinion on some point in connexion with the impeachment, and, on Dundas declining to give it, pressed him saying, "You cannot be indifferent about our success." "Troth, am I," are the words put into the mouth of Dundas by Burges, "ye hae done a' we wanted, and I shall gie mysel' nae trouble aboot what comes o' ye." "Will you say so to any one else?" was Lord Maitland's rejoinder. "Troth, shall I," said Dundas, and repeated, according to Burges, what he had just said to Fitzpatrick and Sheridan, who were also managers. Nothing more need be said about the impeachment for the present, except that, after exciting a wide interest and curiosity, which speedily died away, it ultimately developed into one of the most monstrous acts of injustice, and one of the greatest scandals, in English history.

In 1789 the great prize of the Scottish bar, the office of Lord President of the Court of Session, became vacant, and was offered to Dundas. Dundas, however, could not tear himself away from the excitement and strife of public life, and refused it. It may be assumed from the making of the offer that Pitt now thought that the services of Dundas were no longer necessary to him. Dundas, however, was not of this opinion, as he showed in a long letter to Grenville. "My secession from all political life at this time would be a very fatal step to the strength and hold Government has of Scotland....A variety of circumstances happen to concur in my person to render me a cement of political strength to the present Administration, which, if it were dissolved, would produce very ruinous effects." He went on to state that his situation was growing every day, as he advanced in years, more irksome and disagreeable to him, and took from him every comfort and enjoyment that he had while in Scotland. But he said that, if he gave it up, the Opposition would gain a strength which would be irresistible, and the Treasury and the Home Office, which was presided over by Grenville, would be kept in constant hot water "amidst the jarrings, and jealousies, and counteracting pretensions of the great men of the country." He goes on to add that the loyalty of Ilay Campbell, the Lord Advocate, to the Government, and to himself personally, made it very

3—3

desirable that Campbell should have the office. He con-
cludes by saying that he is not actuated by folly or false
ambition in refusing the post of Lord President. "I assure
you," he says, "the recollection of a Rigby or a Welbore
Ellis are never out of my mind as a warning to leave the
bustle of politics and the House of Commons, before the
vigour of your body and the activity of your mind leave
you."

The real truth of the matter was that Dundas knew
that Pitt and Grenville were too much above the standard
of those around them to do without his help. They were
men with lofty ideals, and ignorant of the arts required to
manage politicians. They were no match for the Whig
magnates, with their rotten boroughs and territorial
influence, or for the Tapers and Tadpoles who did the
work of those magnates. Dundas, on the other hand,
possessed unrivalled political tact and penetrating discernment of character. In the eyes of Robert Burns, he
was "a chap that's damned auldfarran[1]," and the "slee[2]
Dundas." Lord Rosebery describes him as one of the
two most acute political tacticians of his time, George
the Third being the other. Dundas possessed a degree
of political foresight, by which he was able to perceive
almost by intuition the exact chances of party warfare.
Pitt needed the protection of somebody like Dundas, with
his long experience of Parliamentary tactics and strategy,
and Dundas was resolved to give him that protection.

The appointment of the Lord Advocate to the post of
Lord President led to the promotion of Dundas's nephew
and son-in-law, Robert Dundas of Arniston, who was
Solicitor-General. He became Lord Advocate in September, 1789. He was a man of moderate abilities, and,

---

[1] *Anglice*, sagacious.   [2] Sly.

according to Cockburn, a "curiously bad" speaker. In June of next year Dundas surrendered to his nephew his seat in Midlothian, and was himself elected member for the city of Edinburgh, which he represented till he was made a peer in 1802.

Among the subjects which were forced from time to time on the attention of Dundas was the unsatisfactory condition of the Scottish burghs. There had been great dissatisfaction for many years with their management and administration. The members of the councils were self-elected; the revenues were misapplied; the property of many of the burghs had been alienated; some of them were deep in debt. Taxes were sometimes imposed without the authority of Parliament, and every species of petty tyranny was exercised by the magistrates. In 1784 a conference of delegates was held with a view to initiating a movement of reform, and a standing committee was appointed. After an immense amount of evidence had been collected, an attempt was made to induce Dundas to deal with the matter. In spite of former tendencies to reform, Dundas was not at all friendly. As Lord Cockburn pointed out, and justly, any amendment of the condition of the burghs would have endangered his supremacy in Scotland. One of the first results, says Cockburn, would have been to estrange the town council of Edinburgh, which was absolutely subservient to his will, and very corrupt. As Robert Fergusson said of the Provosts of Edinburgh in *Auld Reikie*,

> "For politics are a' their mark,
> Bribes latent, and corruption dark."

Cockburn, after describing the Edinburgh council chamber as a low-roofed room, very dark and very dirty, goes on to picture its occupants in lurid terms. "Within this

pandemonium," he says, "sat the Town Council, omni-
potent, corrupt, impenetrable. Nothing was beyond its
grasp, no variety of opinion disturbed its equanimity, for
the pleasure of Dundas was the sole rule for every one
of them....Silent, powerful, submissive, mysterious, and
irresponsible, they might have been sitting in Venice."
This picture may be a little overdrawn, but there was
certainly some foundation for the charges of corruption
and servility to Dundas. In spite, however, of the
existence of abuses, the Scottish minister would not
favour any measure that endangered his authority in
Scotland or its capital.

Dundas having refused to assist the burgh reformers,
Sheridan eventually undertook to champion their cause,
and certainly showed no lack of zeal in the work. Between
1787 and 1792 he brought the subject before the House
twelve times. In May, 1791, during a debate on the subject,
Dundas admitted the existence of many of the grievances
urged by Sheridan, but pointed out that the Royal burghs
in Scotland had existed since 1469, and that the state of
the English burghs and Stafford, which was represented
by Sheridan, in particular, was quite as bad. Ultimately
the excesses of the French Revolution excited so strong
a feeling against changes of any kind that the promoters
of burgh reform were compelled to abandon their projects
until a more convenient season.

In 1791 Dundas, who was already Treasurer of the
Navy and a member of the Board of Control, obtained a
seat in the Cabinet by his appointment to the office of
Secretary of State for the Home department, his predecessor
Grenville having been appointed to the Foreign department.
The accession of Grenville to the post of Foreign Secretary
was an event of considerable importance in the history of

the Pitt administration, and his character exercised a potent influence on the policy of Pitt. Grenville was very upright, very conscientious, very able, very resolute, very courageous. He was less liberal, less pliant in discussion, and less prone to make expediency the rule of his political conduct than Pitt. He showed himself inflexible even to obstinacy and incapable of compromise on points involving principle or personal conviction. He was unsympathetic, with little sense of humour and singularly small knowledge of men. "I am not competent," he said in a letter to his brother, "to the management of men. I never was so naturally, and toil and anxiety more and more unfit me for it." He was not genial or amiable, but of the type of men that secures esteem without affection. He was probably a sounder scholar than either Pitt or Fox, and spoke French and Italian, and had not neglected Spanish. He had also made a careful study of geography, which was then a rare accomplishment in a cabinet minister. Brougham states that, as a speaker, he dealt chiefly in argument, and that his oratory was clear, impressive, and authoritative. His gifts made him a most useful auxiliary to Pitt, who valued him increasingly, as time went on.

As Home Secretary Dundas received the management of Irish affairs—a charge which then, as now, was an anxious and difficult one. The influence of the French Revolution was making itself widely felt, and was producing in Ireland a spirit of revolt and unrest. The question of Catholic emancipation was being actively pressed, and efforts were being made to unite it with the promotion of Parliamentary Reform. A determined attempt was being made to combine the northern dissenters, who were permeated by democratic, and even republican opinions, with the discontented Catholics.

Dundas was in favour of relief to the Catholics and of giving them the franchise. In view of the conditions in Ireland, however, he had to proceed with great tact and caution. The negotiations that ensued are described by Lecky in his history with fullness and lucidity. His attempts to induce the Irish Government to conciliate the Catholics were received at first with hostility and consternation. "I am convinced," wrote Lord Westmoreland, the Lord Lieutenant, to Pitt, "you might as well attempt to carry in the English Parliament the abolition of negro slavery, a reform of representation, or an abolition of the House of Lords in the House of Lords, as to carry the Irish Parliament a step towards the franchise." The opposition of the Irish Government was so strong that the franchise proposal was abandoned, but only for a time. At the end of the following year the condition of affairs on the continent was so serious that Dundas again urged on the Irish Government the importance of securing the assistance of the Catholics in support of the established constitution. His efforts on this occasion were successful, and in February, 1793, a measure was introduced, by which the franchise and other concessions were granted to the Catholics.

In April of 1793 the question of renewing the monopoly of the East India Company for a further term of years was considered by the House of Commons. There was much opposition to this monopoly, and a strong effort had been made by the merchants of Liverpool, Glasgow, and other commercial communities, to get the trade of India thrown open. Dundas took up a position of strong hostility to those endeavours. He supported the renewal of the exclusive privileges of the Company, declaring that the existing system had worked well hitherto, and that

a change might have a bad effect on the natives.
"I own," he said, "that, next to the interests of my
country, the prosperity of the East India Company, in
the management of whose business I have had my share,
claims my first public regard." His speech on this
occasion was, in the opinion of Pitt, one, which, in its
comprehensive knowledge of the history of India, and
of the various sources of British commerce in the East,
might have been equalled in the House of Commons but
had never been excelled. The charter was ultimately
renewed for twenty years. Shortly after this successful
effort, Dundas became President of the Board of Control.

CHAPTER V

The influence of Dundas in the British cabinet was strengthened and supported by his extraordinary supremacy in Scotland. He "predominated" over Scotland as the Bear of Bradwardine predominated over the stone basin of the fountain at Tullyveolan, and was the source from which flowed all place and power. He enjoyed an unquestioned authority among his own countrymen, while holding an outstanding place in the greater theatre of Westminster. He stood like a Colossus with one foot in London, and one in Edinburgh. To understand the peculiar position of Dundas in Scotland it is necessary to have some knowledge of the methods by which Scottish affairs were administered during the eighteenth century. After the union of the parliaments in 1707 the office of Secretary of State, which had existed in the independent kingdom of Scotland, was retained under the new *régime*, and was continued till the dismissal of the Duke of Roxburgh in 1725, when it was abolished. In 1742 the office was revived, but was finally done away with in 1746, and its formal functions added to those of the English Home Secretary, who was regarded as Secretary for Scotland. Lord Provost Hunter Blair wrote to North in 1783, "I beg leave to address your Lordship as Secretary of State for Scotland."

While the Home Secretary had the nominal control of Scottish administration, the real control of Scotland was handed over to some highly-placed individual, who represented Scotland to the central government, and the central government to Scotland. On the abolition of the Scottish Secretaryship, the reins of power were given to Archibald, third Duke of Argyll, who retained the control of affairs till his death in 1761. Argyll was succeeded in the management of Scotland by his nephew, the Earl of Bute, who was Secretary of State, and who delegated the work of administration to his brother, Stuart Mackenzie. Mackenzie in his turn was succeeded as manager of Scottish affairs by others, who need not be particularised, beyond saying that a good deal of Scottish patronage was informally enjoyed by members of the Dundas family before Henry Dundas appeared on the field. Ultimately, with the gradual strengthening of Dundas's position at Westminster, the control of Scotland passed completely into his hands, and he became the most absolute of all the ministers who had managed the affairs of his native country.

Whoever the manager or dispenser of Scottish patronage might be, his position was autocratic. All administrative and executive posts were filled in conformity with his advice and recommendation. The list of the sixteen Scottish peers at the General Election was dictated by him, and the forty-five representatives in the House of Commons were, for the most part, chosen, if not in obedience to his instructions, at all events with his consent and approbation. He was the sole channel of solicitation to ministers, and all favours passed through his hands. He had generally a *sous-ministre*, who represented him in his absence from Scotland, and kept him in touch with local affairs. When Archibald, Duke of Argyll was minister for Scotland, his delegate was Andrew Fletcher, Lord Milton, the Lord Justice Clerk, a nephew of the patriotic Fletcher of Saltoun. When Stuart Mackenzie was Scottish minister during the *régime* of his brother, the Earl of Bute the *sous-ministre* was Baron Mure of Caldwell. It need hardly be said that the position of Scottish minister lost none of its *prestige*, when its privileges were deputed to subordinates in the Scottish capital. Even appointments, which were nominally in the gift of corporations, or which were presumed to be filled by individuals in virtue of their official or patrimonial privileges, were seldom made without the goodwill of the man in power. Dr Sommerville states, for example, that Lord Provost Drummond did not find himself at liberty to promise any preferment at the disposal of the Town Council of Edinburgh without the previous consent of Lord Milton, the deputy of Archibald, Duke of Argyll.

No one, who aspired to place or power, dreamed of revolting against the autocrat or his delegate. They were the absolute arbiters of the political fortunes of ambitious Scotsmen. It was idle for anybody to appeal to the Scottish members, as Burns did, in his *Earnest Cry and Prayer to the Scotch Representatives in the House of Commons*,

> "Does any great man glunch an' gloom?
> Speak out, an' never fash your thumb!
> Let posts an' pensions sink or soom
> Wi' them wha grant 'em.
> If honestly they canna come,
> Far better want 'em."

A Scottish member of Parliament, who voted against the administration, became a marked man. In 1780 Sir Lawrence Dundas, the member for Edinburgh, with six other Scottish members, supported Dunning in his motion with regard to the increasing power of the Crown. The

result of his vote was that Dundas threw his weight into
the scale against him in the election of the same year,
and he was defeated by Miller, the son of the Lord Justice
Clerk. It was a feature of Scottish administration that
no Englishman was allowed to find a place among Scottish
representatives. Except Chauncey Townshend, member
for Wigton, who died in 1770, no Englishman was returned
for a Scottish constituency for more than half a century
after the Union, and during the rest of the century the
return of an Englishman as a Scottish representative was
quite exceptional. The Parliamentary representation of
Scotland was indeed not only purely national, but even
local and territorial. Members of the same great families
are found representing the same constituencies for long
periods of years. Lord Brougham was probably right in
assuming that the old feudal habits of the nation were at
least one cause of that submission to men in high place,
which was so much more absolute in Scotland than in
England.

The smallness of the electorate made it manageable
and submissive. At the General Election of 1790, when
the power of Dundas was at its height, the number of
county voters in Scotland was 2624. Ayrshire with 220
voters was the largest county constituency, and Cromarty
with 6 votes the smallest. The total number of borough
electors in 1790 was 1289. Edinburgh had a member to
itself, and the other Royal burghs were arranged in
fourteen groups or districts, each returning one member.
The voters in burghs were the town councils, which were
self-elected. They appointed delegates, who met and
chose the member. The limited character of the county
franchise, which was in the hands of the freeholders alone,
led to the wholesale manufacture of votes. Although the

largest landowner in a county could have one vote only, yet by dividing his property into parcels and handing them over in trust only to nominal freeholders, he could enfranchise persons whose votes were practically his own. Attempts were made to stop this practice by legislation, but the provisions of the statutes were eluded. At the time when Pitt came into power, the county constituencies were completely swamped by the "parchment barons," as the nominal freeholders were called. In the county of Moray, the nominal freeholders were to the real free-holders in the proportion of four to one. Cockburn says that the election of either a burgh or county member was a matter of such utter indifference to the people that they often only knew of it by the ringing of a bell, or by see-ing it mentioned next day in a newspaper. Politically Scotland was asleep. It was, says Cockburn, not unlike a village at a great man's gate.

There is constant and abundant proof in Dundas's letters of his close attention to the management of the electors and of the elections. He is found for example writing to the Duke of Rutland, when Lord Lieutenant of Ireland, asking him to get a clergyman in Dublin named Hamilton to vote for Dundas of Dundas in the Midlothian election of 1784. Again in 1786 he writes to the Duke saying that he wants Colonel Knight of the Forty-fifth regiment to vote for Ferguson of Pitfour in Aberdeenshire. He was ready to use personal solicitation, where he considered it would be useful. In a letter of 2nd September, 1787, he writes to Lord Grenville from Athole House,

"I am this far on my way to the North of Scotland on a visit to Sir James Grant, General Grant, Duke of Gordon, Lord Findlater, and Lord Fife. They are all very hostile to each other; and yet I am told that a visit from me may probably have the effect of uniting their political interests in such a manner as to co-operate for securing five seats in Parliament at the general election in the interest of the government; whereas, if I do not interpose, there is a danger of their getting into immediate warfare among themselves, and, if that happens, it is a throw of the dice how their competitions may ultimately end.''

Much light is thrown on the electioneering methods of the time by a report, which was presented to the Right Honourable William Adam, who, with Henry Erskine, managed the interests in Scotland of the Whig opposition to the administration of Pitt and Dundas. The report is a roll of the Scottish county electors of 1788, with a statement of their objects, connexions, and circumstances —all very valuable information to a party manager. The roll is a remarkable testimony to the power of Dundas. It is interesting to look through the list of voters for the county of Midlothian, which he himself represented. Robert Dundas of Arniston is described as having a considerable estate, and good interest, and as being able to make a good many votes. Dundas himself is stated to be able to make three votes on his own estate. Of the ninety-three voters, who made up the electorate for the county, ten are stated to be indebted to Dundas. The particulars of those ten voters contained in the report are worth reproducing, and are as follows:

(26) Archibald Cockburn, Sheriff of the County. "Has been made Judge Admiral through Mr Dundas.''

(30) John Davidson of Haltree, W.S. "Has been obliged to Mr Dundas, to whom he is Deputy Keeper to the Signet.''

(32) James, Count Lockhart of Lee. "His brother lately appointed to an office in the Customs at Bo'ness through the Duke of Hamilton and Mr Dundas.''

(39) John Russell of Roseburn, W.S. "Has a son who was made Agent for Teinds through Mr Dundas.''

(53)   Charles Gordon of Braid, W.S.   "Made a Clerk of Session through Mr Dundas and the Duke of Gordon."
(58)   Sir Archibald Hope of Pinkie.   "His son-in-law once in Mr Dundas's office."
(63)   Robert Baird of Newbyth.   "Under obligations to Mr Dundas."
(64)   Mark Pringle, Esq.   "Collector of the Crown Rents through the interest of the Duke of Buccleugh and Mr Dundas."
(79)   James Gillespie of Spylaw.   "A tobacconist in Edinburgh.   Very rich.   Mr Dundas lately got a presentation from Lord Elphinstone to a minister recommended by him."
(83)   Samuel Mitchelson of Clermiston, W.S.   "Lately made a Clerk of Session by Mr Dundas."

Of the seventy-five voters in Haddingtonshire, Dundas himself had a life-rent vote from the Duke of Buccleugh, and his nephew and son-in-law, Robert Dundas, had also a vote.   No less than four of the voters had married nieces of Dundas; Hamilton of Pencaitland, Buchan of Kello, Colt of Scougal, and Sir John Ross of Balnagowan. Two of the voters, Robert Sinclair, advocate, and George Home of Branxton, had been appointed Clerks of Session by Dundas.   Sir John Sinclair of Murkle was a relation of Dundas.   Robert Baird of Newbyth is "under obliga-tions to Dundas."   Thomas Broun of Johnstonburn is "obliged to Dundas."   Charles Brown of Coalston is "connected with Dundas."   Sir James Murray of Hillhead is "an intimate of Dundas's."   James Veitch of Caponflat "will go with Dundas."   Alexander Mackenzie of Seton, W.S., "will not like to oppose Mr Dundas."

Dundas exercised upon his countrymen all the little arts and devices of popularity, which even the lofty mind of Burke did not disdain.   "They facilitate," said Burke, "the carrying of many points of moment; they keep the people together; they refresh the mind in its exertions; and they diffuse occasional gaiety over the severe brow of moral freedom." Dundas knew how to manage his fellow countrymen, and was quick to discern and attract adherents. He kept his eye, like Disraëli, on young men of promise. His nephew, Robert, when Lord Advocate, kept open house for the younger members of the Scottish landed classes, and, by his hospitality and kindness, did much to attract them to the support of the government. Scattered over Scotland, as over all countries with any pretence to freedom, were men who guided local opinion and controlled each his little orb—the popular provost, the hospitable laird, the active writer, the eloquent preacher.

> "Multum in Fabiâ valet hic, valet ille Velinâ;
> Cuilibet hic fasces dabit eripietque curule."

Dundas kept closely in touch with men of this type, and used them to maintain his influence and supremacy. On the Scottish metropolis, in particular, he kept a watchful eye. Lockhart says that there was no person of any consideration in Edinburgh, whose whole connexions and concerns were not perfectly well known to Dundas. A letter taken almost at random shows how firm was his hold. In September, 1799, Lord Provost Stirling writes to him, "On this you may confidently rely, that no person whatever shall, with my consent, be admitted into the council, who is not, to the best of my knowledge and belief, not only correct in his political principles, but also firmly attached to your interest."

The authority which Dundas was able to exercise in Scotland was rendered possible by his thorough knowledge of his countrymen. It was said by Bishop Burnet of Lord Shaftesbury in the seventeenth century, that his strength lay in his knowledge of England, and it may be said with equal truth of Dundas that his strength lay in his knowledge of Scotland. Dundas knew his countrymen completely, and was in the utmost sympathy with their most characteristic traits. He always remained a Scotsman to the backbone. He was not an Anglicised Scot like Lord Mansfield; he was entirely Scottish in all respects. To the Londoners he was "Scotch Harry," always depicted in the caricatures—absurdly enough—in kilt and tartan. He spoke with a broad Scottish accent which he never attempted to soften.

"Full weil his ain dear Scotch he'd speak,"
says the *Melviad.* "His oratory was indeed very fine," Lord George Gordon once said, "Lingua Tuscana in voce Romana." There was a great ambition on the part of the Scottish politicians of that day to divest themselves of their native notes. Lord Mansfield contrived to get rid of his accent, although Lord Shelburne says that he always spoke "in a feigned voice like Leoni the Jew singer." Wedderburn took extraordinary pains to acquire the English method of pronunciation, as his biographer, Lord Campbell, relates in a piquant chapter. Boswell took lessons in utterance and delivery from Love of Drury Lane, and from Thomas Sheridan, the father of the statesman, and was gratified when Johnson said to him, "Sir, your pronunciation is not offensive." Dundas never betrayed any ambition to acquire an English accent, and clung to the speech and tones of his native land.

In the House of Commons the peculiarities of his speech often afforded amusement. But it was pointed out by more than one writer that his broad accent was not without its advantages. Boswell says that it raised the attention of the House by its uncommonness and was equal to tropes and figures in a good English speaker. Wraxall alleges that his defects of elocution or diction, "by the ludicrous effect that they produced, became often converted into advantages; as they unavoidably operated to force a smile from his bitterest opponents and chequered with momentary good humour the personalities of debate." The friends of Dundas sometimes teased him about his quaint northern expressions. On one occasion, using a common Scotticism, he asked Pitt for the loan of a horse, "the length of Highgate." Pitt replied that he was afraid that he had not a horse quite so long as Dundas mentioned, but he had sent the longest he had.

A strange gibberish was sometimes put into the mouth of Dundas by the lampooners of the day. In a skit, to take one specimen, published in 1785, entitled *Probationary Odes for the Laureateship*, the vacancy in the post of laureate was supposed to have called forth a host of rivals to Thomas Warton, who was ultimately appointed. Each of his Majesty's ministers enters into the competition, and contributes an ode more or less characteristic of himself. Dundas is supposed to say in his contribution,

"Hoot! hoot awaw!
Hoot! hoot, awaw!
Ye lawland bards! who are ye aw?
What are your sangs? what aw your lair to boot?
Vain are your thowghts the prize to win,
Sae dight your gobs, and stint your senseless din;
Hoot! hoot awaw! hoot! hoot!
Put oot aw your attic feires,
Burn your lutes, and brek your leyres;
A looder and a looder note I'll streike:—
Na watter drawghts fra Helicon I heed,
Na will I moont your winged steed,—
I'll moont the Hanoverian horse, and ride him whare I leike."

Dundas was the most absolute of any minister that ever controlled Scottish administration. He was "king of

Scotland" in a far truer sense than John, Duke of Argyll, to whom that epithet had been given at an earlier period of the century, had ever been. Argyll had always been opposed and often with success. Stuart Mackenzie also was thwarted and disobeyed. Writing to Baron Mure, he said, in a moment of irritation, that there was no country in Europe where the want of obedience was almost universal except Scotland. Dundas for many years was seldom opposed and almost never with success. His power was increased by the absence, during his earlier career, of Party feeling in Scotland. During the greater part of the eighteenth century the struggles of English politicians and the continued scuffle between the government and the opposition were regarded by the people of Scotland with indifference. Except during the brief tenure of power secured by Bute, the leaders of the Parties were for the most part English magnificoes in whom Scotland could feel no interest. What did it matter to Scotland whether the Duke of Grafton or the Marquis of Rockingham rose or fell? Something of this feeling was exhibited before the Union by the Scottish statesman, Fletcher of Saltoun, when he proposed that the patronage of Scotland should be taken out of the hands of the Sovereign, and exercised in the Scottish Parliament by ballot. When some of the courtiers spoke of the project as republican, Fletcher said that it merely transferred the power of governing Scotland from a knot of English placemen to the national representatives. Apart from the Jacobite element, the balance of moderate opinion in Scotland gave a general support to the successive ministries of Walpole and the Pelhams and Chatham. Loyalty to the Crown and to the ministers enjoying the confidence of the Crown was the guiding principle. It was not until the last decade of the century that Scotland became definitely divided into Whig and Tory. This Scottish indifference to Party badges undoubtedly had its influence on Dundas himself, and the readiness with which he passed from one administration to another is partly explainable on this basis.

CHAPTER VI

In 1793 a very important event in the history of Pitt's administration took place; war broke out between Great Britain and France. During all the excesses and violence of the French Revolution, Pitt had persistently preached peace, and refrained from interference. But, to use a phrase of Burke, the coming war slept in the thin ashes of the seeming peace. When Louis the Sixteenth was executed, a thrill of horror ran through Great Britain, and the continuance of friendly relations became no longer possible. War was declared, and from that time Pitt knew no rest from work and anxiety. No thought of himself, however, or of his own ease ever abated his hostility to the spirit of Revolution, or shook his determination that the crest of Great Britain should never be lowered in face of her enemies. His tenacity, his determination, his courage, never wavered as long as life remained.

It is not the intention of the writer to say much on a story so often told as that of the long contest with France. Pitt's difficulties in conducting the struggle were greatly increased by his profound ignorance of war, and the equally profound ignorance of Dundas, who, as Home Secretary, was responsible for military operations. There was no Marlborough to pit against the genius of Carnot and Napoleon. Beyond the exhibition of British resolution and persistence which it afforded, the military record of the nation, while Pitt was minister, can arouse no pride or satisfaction. The British commanders could boast of no brilliant exploits, and could claim no laurels for striking achievements. There were many occasions when the words of Hardy in his fine play, *The Dynasts,* were only too true.

"Feebly-framed dull unresolve, unresourcefulness,
  Sat in the halls of the kingdom's high Councillors,
  Whence the grey glooms of a ghost-eyed despondency
  Wanned as with winter the national mind."

Mr Fortescue, in his brilliant history of the British Army, has spoken of Dundas, as war minister, in the severest and most unsparing terms. He describes him as a "deplorable impostor," and denounces his "extreme incapacity," his "insufferable conceit," his "incurable negligence even of the most elementary military arrangements," his unwise interference with the generals in the field, his "criminal carelessness," "the incoherence and folly of his orders," his lack of courtesy, his tendency to bluster, when he was proved to be in the wrong. Speaking of one outburst of Dundas to Abercromby, Mr Fortescue says that the charitable explanation would be that Dundas was drunk when he penned it, but, says Mr Fortescue, "if drunkenness be accepted in excuse of his innumerable foolish actions, the conclusion must inevitably follow that he was very rarely sober." When the British ought, according to Mr Fortescue, to have helped the gallant insurgents of La Vendée, they wasted time and money on the useless siege of Dunkirk. When the French Royalists handed over to them the great fortress of Toulon, and the ministers ought, in Mr Fortescue's view, to have thrown into it every soldier they could spare,

they sent large bodies of troops to die like flies from
yellow fever in the West Indies.

Any historical judgment, enunciated by Mr Fortescue,
is entitled to the greatest weight. It is easy to see that
many blunders were made. There was no coordination
of diplomatic policy and strategy, no organisation of the
Higher Direction. The military operations of Great
Britain frequently exhibited miscalculation, wavering
purpose, and ineffectual action. Yet when all is said,
one cannot help feeling that Mr Fortescue is too unsparing
in his condemnation of Dundas, and too severe in his
judgments. Mr Julian Corbett, in his introduction to
the first volume of the *Spencer Papers*, after referring to
Mr Fortescue's strictures, puts in a word for the War
minister. "Those," says Mr Corbett, "who read his un-
daunted and well-reasoned letters to Lord Spencer, and
especially those in which he protests against excessive
concentration in Home waters and against abandoning
the Mediterranean, will feel that the man was not all
shallow self-confidence and heady miscalculation—that
he had at least on occasion an eye for the great lines of
a war and kept at any rate a stout heart that would not
despair of his country." Mr Corbett expresses strong
sympathy with the passion for offence, which his policy
displayed. Speaking of the plans to repel French invasion
in the last years of the eighteenth century, Mr Corbett
says that, like his master, Chatham, Dundas held that to
sit down and await attack was the one unpardonable sin.
His master note was to seize every half chance to strike,
and, if striking was not possible, to try to scratch. This,
whenever he found a finger free, he was prepared to do.
He has been ridiculed for it on military grounds, says
Mr Corbett, but, as the *Spencer Papers* show, the grounds

on which he based his policy were not purely military. It was to the moral effect he mainly looked; and to this end he was prepared to risk much, so long as he could give heart to his country, maintain its offensive spirit, and worry the shaky revolutionary government with a perpetual menace of attack. It should be added that Mr Corbett's view that Mr Fortescue is too vehement in his censures of Dundas, is shared by another eminent historian, Dr Holland Rose.

It has been alleged as a reason for blaming Dundas that he looked to the effect upon public opinion of his military operations. Mr Fortescue complains that he regarded the war from the electioneering point of view, and that he increased the difficulties of the situation by this habit. He tried to do, says Mr Fortescue, what would please the people at the next election. When he was persuaded by the Royalist refugees to occupy the French West Indies, and the wealthy island of San Domingo in particular, the project pleased him, because he saw that it would revive memories of Chatham, and would be a good advertisement. It would gratify the public, and would bring money into the Exchequer and trade to Great Britain. He did not foresee, says Mr Fortescue, how costly in human lives it would be, and how worthless from the point of view of disabling France. Yet it is interesting to observe that, while it appears to be generally agreed that the failure of the British policy to deal with the Revolution in its early stages was mainly due to the absorption and wastage of troops in the West Indies, Mr Corbett expresses the opinion that it is by no means easy to see how this strategical error could have been avoided. In any case Dundas, in carrying on the war, was compelled to consider and keep right with popular opinion. If the nation was to remain willing to support the great strain of the war, it had to be studied and humoured. Even Napoleon at times did not hesitate to play to the gallery in the conduct of his military operations.

It has been said by some writers that Pitt had no great generals on whom he could rely. Grenville complained that, when he wanted a commander, he could only find "some old woman in a red riband." Mr Fortescue protests against this suggestion as unjust and unfair, and in this he secures our sympathy. Ralph Abercromby, Charles Grey, Lord Cornwallis, Lord Moira, Charles Stuart, John Moore, Arthur Wellesley, were all able and competent generals. It was Pitt and Dundas who never gave them a chance. It was the old women in the red ribands in the cabinet, says Mr Fortescue, that were the real culprits. When handfuls of untrained troops were sent on foolish and impossible enterprises, the British commanders wholly lost all trust and confidence in the government. "There are risks in a British warfare," wrote Ralph Abercromby to Dundas, "unknown in any other service." As Mr Fortescue has said, the British commanders proved capable enough, when they were entrusted with forces of decent strength. It was not until the Duke of York was placed at the head of the army in 1795 that it was rescued from disorder and chaos. As Mr Fortescue says, only those who know the history of the army intimately before his time can appreciate the service that the Duke of York rendered to his country.

The strain of the war forced upon Pitt's attention the desirability of strengthening his cabinet from the ranks of the Opposition. The leaders of the aristocratic section of the Whigs were induced—very much to the disgust and annoyance of Fox—to take office under him. In

July, 1794, the Duke of Portland became Secretary of State, Earl Spencer, Lord Privy Seal, Earl Fitzwilliam, President of the Council, and Windham, Secretary at War with a seat in the cabinet[1]. At the time of this junction of forces Dundas was Secretary of State with charge of Home, Colonial and Military affairs. Pitt revived the third Secretaryship of State, which had been abolished in 1782, and divided the duties of the office, which Dundas held between Dundas and Portland. When the new arrangement was made Pitt had intended that Dundas should continue to have charge of Colonial and Military affairs, while Portland should have charge of Home affairs. As a result of some misunderstanding, however, it appeared that Portland expected to control all that the Secretary of State had previously controlled except the war. Dundas was ready to give way, but, hurt and wounded by Pitt's apparent disregard of his feelings and interests, he declared that he would retire from the Secretaryship and the conduct of the war. Pitt in the greatest distress wrote a most urgent and pressing letter to Dundas, saying that he would be "really completely heart-broken," if Dundas adhered to his resolution. He asked Dundas to remain in office, as the strongest proof he could give him of friendship to himself. Dundas still refused to accede to Pitt's wish, and Pitt went to the King and obtained a letter from him in which the King called on Dundas in the strongest manner to continue Secretary of State for War. Going with this letter to Dundas, whom he found at dinner with his family, Pitt again made an urgent appeal to him, and at last induced him to remain in office.

The task of government, after the commencement of

[1] A different office from Secretary of State for War.

the war, was made infinitely more difficult by the extension
of the revolutionary spirit from France to Great Britain.
Organisations were founded to promote reform and
advocate the extension of popular rights. Pitt, although
still in principle a reformer, declared that it was no time
for "hazardous experiments," and a policy of repression
was entered upon at home, concurrently with the war
abroad. The proclamation against seditious writings,
the suspension of the Habeas Corpus Act in 1794, annually
renewed until 1801, the Treasonable Practices Act, the
Seditious Meetings Act in 1795, the increase of the stamp
duties with a view to crushing heap newspapers, the
suppression of associations like the London Corresponding
Society, gradually withdrew fron the nation a great part
of the liberty it had previously enjoyed. The policy of
repression was accompanied by bad harvests, and by heavy
taxation, high prices, unemployment, and all the evils
following on an unsuccessful war. It is not surprising
that great discontent and unrest ensued, and that men,
with anything to lose, lived in terror of a revolution and
a repetition in England of the horrors in France. It was
during this period that all the dreams of reform, once
nourished by Pitt, were driven from his mind, and that
Toryism, of which he was now regarded as the protagonist,
unfortunately became identified with a fear of concession to
popular liberties and a belief that coercion was a necessary
instrument of government. The political ideals of Swift
and Bolingbroke disappeared, to remain in abeyance till
Canning commenced, and Disraeli completed, the task of
restoring to Toryism its popular vigour and national
sympathies.

In Dundas's "kingdom" of Scotland the revolutionary
spirit was even more pronounced than in England. The

circulation of Paine's famous work, *The Rights of Man*, the opposition of the government to burgh reform, the Corn Bill of 1791 for encouraging the exportation and restraining the importation of corn, and other causes, combined to produce what Burke called a rank luxuriance of sedition. In the middle of the year 1792, the effigy of Dundas was burnt in Aberdeen, Perth, Dundee, and many other places. On the King's birthday in June, 1792, there were serious riots in Edinburgh, and the houses of the Lord Advocate and the Lord Provost were attacked. Letters poured in upon Dundas, all telling the same story of Democratic Clubs, Trees of Liberty, disturbances and riots. When Dundas went to Scotland in October, the alarm was so great that he was scarcely suffered to leave the country. "If I was to give way," he wrote to Nepean in December, "to the importunity and anxiety of those who wish to retain my assistance here, I would never get away." In 1793 Thomas Muir, an advocate in Edinburgh, and Palmer, a Unitarian minister in Dundee, were tried for sedition and sentenced to long periods of transportation. In 1794 the same thing happened to Skirving, Margarot, and Gerald. These persons were men of the type, described by Burke, to whom a state of order was a sentence of obscurity, and who were nourished into a dangerous magnitude by the ferment of discontent. But the severity of the treatment meted out to them made them objects of sympathy. The judge, who presided over their trials, was the notorious Robert MacQueen, Lord Braxfield, the Lord Justice Clerk, who has been described by the vivid pen of Cockburn, and who lives in the page of romance as "Weir of Hermiston." In the performance of his office, he displayed such violence, and such flagrant political bias, that great disgust was excited among all fair-minded men. Dundas himself was furiously attacked in Parliament, and Mr Omond says that never, except on one memorable occasion, did any Scottish official sit in the House of Commons through such a storm of reprobation.

While prosecuting the advocates of revolution, Dundas endeavoured to enlist the support of the Conservative elements in the country. The ministers of the Established Church, both Moderates and Evangelicals, and the Dissenting Presbyterian ministers were assiduously cultivated. The first Secession Minister to obtain a doctorate in Divinity, which he received from Aberdeen, was Young of Hawick, who had written an anti-democratic pamphlet. The former loyalty of the Scottish Episcopalian and Roman Catholic Churches to the Stuart princes proved their bias towards the principle of authority, and the members of both communions were relieved from the religious disabilities under which they lay; the former in 1792, and the latter in 1793. The government even made grants to the Roman Catholic priests and seminaries in Scotland. The aid of the press was also invoked. The *Edinburgh Herald* was supported out of the Secret Service Fund, and various writers in the *Caledonian Mercury* seem to have been remunerated. Dundas established one Brown of Dundee, the author of a pamphlet, *Look before ye Loup, by Tam Thrum, an Auld Weaver*, as editor of a government organ in Edinburgh, called the *Patriots' Weekly Chronicle*.

The determination of Dundas to resist the spread of what he believed to be a revolutionary spirit was shown by his conduct to Henry Erskine, who had succeeded him as Lord Advocate in the Portland ministry. In 1795 two bills were proposed, one to stop seditious meetings more effectually, and the other to ensure the safety of

the King, who had been attacked in October, 1795.
A public meeting was held to protest against those bills,
at which Henry Erskine took a prominent part. It
happened that Erskine, who was a man of remarkable
gifts, striking eloquence, and great popularity, held the
office of Dean of the Faculty of Advocates in which he
had succeeded Dundas himself in 1785, and which made
him *doyen* of the Scottish bar. His action so irritated
Dundas that he took steps to ensure his rejection, when
he came up for re-election as Dean in January, 1796.
Robert Dundas, the Lord Advocate, was chosen in his
stead. This occurrence created a great sensation throughout Scotland, and elicited some doggerel stanzas from
Burns.

> "Dire was the hate at old Harlaw,
>   That Scot to Scot did carry;
> And dire the discord Langside saw,
>   For beauteous, hapless Mary;
>
> But Scot with Scot ne'er met so hot,
>   Or were more in fury seen, Sir,
> Than 'twixt Hal and Bob for the famous job,
>   Who should be Faculty's Dean, Sir."

With the repressive measures of Dundas, and his
opposition to any measures of reform, the lines of party
in Scotland became more and more acute. Up to the
last decade of the century, most Scotsmen, who were
not Jacobites gave a general adhesion to the doctrines of
the Revolution Whigs. But with the gradual establishment of the power of Dundas, the Whig opponents of
the government drew themselves increasingly apart, and
acquired a distinct creed and organisation of their own.
The appearance of definite party divisions was accompanied by a development of bitter party feeling. Cockburn,
speaking of the last decade of the century, says that

never, since the Revolution in Scotland, had there been a period when public life was so exasperated by hatred, or the charities of private life so soured by political aversion. Party feeling threw its blight even over the broad and genial mind of Scott, who yet himself realised the hurtfulness of its influence. "Tory and Whig may go be damned together," he once said, "as names that have disturbed old Scotland, and torn asunder the most kindly feelings, since the first day they were invented. Yes, damn them, they are the spells to rouse all our angry passions."

The Tory party in Scotland came to be identified—and that much more than in England—with hostility to reform. Pitt and Dundas had both commenced their political life as Whigs, and yet it was their policy that was responsible for this regrettable result. It was impossible to defend the management of burghs by self-elected magistrates, who refused the burgesses any control over their own money. It was urgently desirable that the franchise should be broadened, "so as to let the industrious farmer and manufacturer," as George Dempster of Dunnichen said, "share at least in a privilege now engrossed by the great lord, the drunken laird, and the drunkener baillie." But, with the horrors of Paris in their minds, the country gentlemen of the type described by Scott in the novels dealing with his own time, the Sir Arthur Wardours and the Sir Robert Hazlewoods, who formed the backbone of the Tory party, shrunk apprehensively from any suggestion of change or innovation. The Tory *régime* of Dundas, who had once been ready to welcome reform, became synonymous with repression and restraint. "Public virtue," says Burke, "being of a nature magnificent and splendid, instituted for great things, and conversant about great concerns, requires abundant scope and room, and cannot spread and grow under confinement, and in circumstances straitened, narrow, and sordid." Public virtue could not thrive, while Dundas, like a Colossus, overshadowed the national life.

It is due to the *régime* of Dundas that Scotland has remained so largely thirled to the Liberal Party. The hostility to the improvement of municipal administration, in particular, especially embittered the people. The teaching of Bolingbroke had shown how loyalty to the Crown and respect for ancient institutions and the other ideals of Toryism could be identified with respect for popular rights, and the redress of abuses and anomalies. Disraeli was to teach the same lesson in later years. If Dundas could have followed in the footsteps of Bolingbroke, the political history of Scotland would certainly have been different. The Radicalism of 1793 was, as Scott again and again asserts, a safer and less disorderly element than the Radicalism of 1816, and would have been much more easily dealt with. If the Tory Party, as Cockburn says, had taken the gradual reformation of existing evils into their own hands, they might have altered and strengthened the foundations of their power. They might have substituted public virtue and popular support for governmental repression and hostility to improvement. They might have secured a much larger share than they have enjoyed in the political life of Scotland. To this day the successors of the Tory Party in Scotland feel the effects of the failure of Dundas to rid himself of the dread inspired by the French Revolution.

CHAPTER VII

On the 23rd of April, 1795, the Hastings trial, which had long ceased to create any public interest, came to an end with the acquittal of Hastings. When Hastings left the bar of the House of Lords, his fortune had been exhausted by the expenses of the trial, and he was almost a ruined man. The directors of the East India Company proposed to repay to Hastings all the legal costs of his trial, and to settle on him a pension of five thousand pounds a year. Dundas, however, as President of the Board of Control, still maintained his hostile attitude towards Hastings, and refused to give his consent. There was a long controversy, which resulted in a compromise. The Company was permitted to grant Hastings an annuity of four thousand pounds, and to advance to him a sum of money without interest. He lived till 1818, when he died at the age of eighty-five.

If Dundas was an unsuccessful war minister, there was one matter in which he showed both wisdom and foresight. He early realised the strategical and commercial importance of the Cape of Good Hope, and its value as a station on the way to our Eastern empire. In 1797 he expressed to Lord Spencer his conviction that it was the key to the commerce of India and China. It was he who was mainly responsible for its annexation to Great Britain. He called the Cape Colony his "favourite child," and watched over its welfare with unflagging zeal. When Lord

Macartney was appointed the first British governor, Dundas selected as the governor's secretary Andrew Barnard, who had married Lady Anne Lindsay, the authoress of *Auld Robin Gray*. Lady Anne, who was the daughter of James, fifth Earl of Balcarres, had not married till she was forty-three years of age, and was fifteen years older than her husband. She had .long been on friendly terms with Dundas, and in the interval between his divorcing his first wife and his marriage with the second, he had been a welcome and frequent visitor in Berkeley Square, where Lady Anne lived with her widowed sister, Lady Margaret Fordyce. There is little doubt that Lady Anne was attached to Dundas, and hoped that he would ask her to become his wife. It was not until Dundas dashed her hopes by his second marriage that she consented to accept one of the numerous offers of marriage that she had received.

It was only after frequent solicitation on the part of Lady Anne Barnard that Dundas gave an appointment to her husband, and, when he did, he seems to have relied more on the wife than the husband. Lord Macartney, the Governor, was not taking his wife out with him, and Lady Anne would be the first lady of the Colony. There was much discontent and veiled hostility to British rule at the Cape, and Dundas knew how invaluable would be the tact, charm, and rare social qualities of the Secretary's wife. He charged her to conciliate the Dutch as much as possible, and write him freely about everything. Lady Anne did write him a large number of interesting letters, which throw a valuable light on the conditions of the Colony at the time. Dundas tied the letters up together, and kept them carefully preserved among his most cherished papers at Melville Castle, which shows that he kept a soft corner in his heart for his old friend. Lady Anne Barnard returned to England in 1802 on the restoration of the Colony to the Dutch. When the Cape was again conquered by the British in 1806, Barnard went out for the second time as Secretary to the Governor, but he died in the following year.

During the last two years of the century, the project of union between Great Britain and Ireland was one of the most important questions of the day. Pitt had come to the conclusion that the only practical solution of the constitutional and administrative difficulties and anomalies inherent in the existing system was the union of the Parliaments. In order to secure the support of the Roman Catholics, hopes of Catholic emancipation were held out by Lord Cornwallis, the Lord Lieutenant. Dundas, who was the warmest friend of the Catholics in the ministry, strongly supported the measure. He maintained that the root of the diseased condition of Ireland was that there was no real confidence between the mass of the people and the Protestant Parliament, that the whole power of the country was vested in one-fourth of the people, and that that one-fourth was separated from the other three-fourths by religious distinction, heightened and envenomed by ancient and hereditary animosities. He believed that an incorporating union was the only safe and efficacious remedy to cure this state of things, and that it would give Ireland a power over the executive and general policy of the Empire, which would far more than compensate her for the loss of her separate legislature. He dwelt in one of his speeches on the good results that had followed from the amalgamation of the English and Scottish Parliaments. He read to the House of Commons the peroration of the famous speech of Lord Belhaven in the Scottish Parliament against the union with England, and showed, point by point, how every prediction of evil had been falsified. He showed how all the elements of Scottish prosperity had developed under the influence of the union, and how the feeling of hostility to it, which once undoubtedly existed, had completely subsided. He suggested that the union with Ireland would enable the British Parliament to do those things for Ireland, which the Irish Parliament could not do for itself, and he pointed out on one occasion that the Scottish union with England led the way to the repeal of the heritable jurisdictions, which the Parliament of Scotland would never have done of itself. The union was duly carried, and the first Imperial Parliament met in January, 1801.

On 10th June, 1800, Dundas was appointed Keeper of the Privy Seal of Scotland. He was now, however, beginning to tire of affairs of State, and his health was beginning to break down under the burden he had carried so long. There is a time, says Burke, when the weather-beaten vessels of the State ought to come into harbour, and Dundas was longing for a rest. For some years the war with France and other troubles had made his life one of constant anxiety. His existence had become what Disraeli called "a closely watched slavery mocked by the name of power." The pressure of anxiety is to be seen in his letters again and again, casting a shadow over his daily life. *Post equitem sedet atra cura*, or, as Sir Walter Scott has paraphrased the line,

> "Still though the headlong cavalier,
> O'er rough and smooth in wild career,
> Seems racing with the wind;
> His sad companion,—ghastly pale,
> And darksome as a widow's veil,
> Care—keeps his seat behind."

Sir John Sinclair records that he stayed overnight with Dundas on the last day of 1795. Early next morning he entered Dundas's room, according to the Scottish custom, and wished him a happy new year. Dundas replied with some emotion after a short pause, "I hope this year will be happier than the last, for I scarcely recollect having spent one happy day in the whole of it." Dundas, unlike Pitt, laboured under the disadvantage of not being a good sleeper. It is said that Pitt, however violent might have been the previous agitation of his mind, never failed to sink into profound repose in a very few minutes after he laid his head on the pillow. Dundas, on the other hand, often lay awake at night, worrying over the troubles of the day. In April, 1800, Dundas wrote to Pitt begging him, if an opportunity occurred, to release him from the oversight of the war. In this letter as in others he complained that he had lost the capacity for sound sleep, and that his rest was always broken, and depended more or less on the current transactions of the day.

Another important factor in making Dundas desire for a cessation of his labours was the decline of his influence with Pitt during the last two or three years of the century. Many historical writers speak as if the friendship of Pitt and Dundas lasted unbroken till the death of the first. Even Wraxall speaks of the pre-eminence, which Dundas obtained in Pitt's regard, as having only terminated with their joint lives. This assumption is not borne out by the facts. There can be no doubt that, towards the end of the century, the influence of Dundas over Pitt began to wane, and he gradually slipped from the high position in Pitt's estimation, which he had so long enjoyed. The principal reason was the hold which Grenville, the Foreign Secretary, steadily obtained on the mind of the Prime

Minister. When Grenville assumed the direction of foreign affairs, he had done so at the urgent request and for the convenience of Pitt. He had not studied European politics, and had not counteracted the defects of an insular education by foreign travel. He distrusted himself and his capacities, and was acutely conscious of his own deficiencies. During the earlier years of the revolutionary war his influence in shaping foreign policy was not equal to that of Dundas, and at the private conferences at Holwood or Wimbledon, it was Dundas, and not Grenville, who, in case of difference, carried the day. But as time went on, the influence of Grenville with Pitt steadily increased. His great abilities, his unwearied application, his conscientious performance of his duties, began to tell. With experience came self-confidence and a desire to have his own way. In the end those qualities, combined with the strength of his convictions, and his tenacity in adhering to them regardless of personal consequences, his conspicuous success as leader of the House of Lords, the presence in the Cabinet of the Portland Whigs, who were, on most questions, in much closer accord with himself than Dundas, and the failure of Dundas to cope with revolutionary energy and enthusiasm, gradually raised him to a position in the Ministry immediately next to that of Pitt. During the last three years of Pitt's administration he seems to have been able to make his own views prevail in the Cabinet in all important questions of external policy. In 1797 Lord Malmesbury and Canning are found wondering at the extraordinary deference Pitt paid to Grenville's opinion. Two years later Dundas had sunk so much in the estimation of his colleagues as to have become a subject of irreverent jest. In December, 1799, Pitt wrote to Grenville in reference to some plan of the Secretary for War, "Dundas's geography, you will observe, is as accurate as his language." Dundas was not a proficient in grammar[1].

Dundas might have secured some relief from his anxieties, if he had accepted a peerage. He seems, however, at this time to have been averse to that idea. In a conversation with Lord Minto in 1798 he said that he considered a peerage a disqualification for "the most flattering and important situations in this country," and that it would exclude his descendants from such situations. Lord Minto urged, on the other hand, that "it would place his descendants in so advantageous a position as to consideration, and even as to political views, that nothing but the most soaring ambition, and the determination to be first minister, could well be frustrated by it." It is interesting to note that already in 1798 a peerage was considered as likely to prove a disqualification for the premiership. In 1800 the weary minister was relieved of some portion of his labours by resigning the offices of Treasurer of the Navy and President of the Board of Control. The directors of the East India Company offered him a pension of two thousand pounds a year, which he declined. But at the same time, with characteristic acuteness, he signified that, if the annuity were granted to his wife, who was considerably younger than himself, it would be accepted; and it was granted accordingly.

The end of the first Pitt administration was now approaching, but, before he went out of office, Dundas obtained a good deal of *kudos*, which Mr Fortescue says was quite undeserved, from Sir Ralph Abercromby's successful operations in Egypt. It is related that Dundas

[1] For example, he writes, "I have wrote," and " You was."

used afterwards to tell with pride how the King breakfasted with him at Wimbledon after the expedition, and proposed a toast to "the minister who planned the expedition to Egypt, and, in doing so, had the courage to oppose his King." He used to add that, when he heard this, he felt as if amends were made to him for all the crosses he had experienced in his life. Mr Fortescue, however always severe, says that the enterprise was one of the most desperate character, and was only undertaken by Abercromby with the greatest reluctance. He was tormented by anxiety and apprehension to the end, and it was only Menou's blunders that crowned the expedition with unexpected success. "Dundas," says Mr Fortescue, "true to his nature, ordered the troops upon an errand which, according to all human calculation, should have ended certainly in failure and possibly in disgrace. Let not, therefore, the Egyptian expedition be taken as in the slightest degree atoning for his previous faults, for it was dictated by precisely the same ignorance, folly, and presumption, as had inspired all his previous enterprises."

On 14th March, 1801, the long ministry of Pitt came to an end. He resigned, and was succeeded by Addington, who was Speaker of the House of Commons. There has been much discussion as to Pitt's reasons for his step, but it is clear that he really retired over the question of Catholic Emancipation. The King would not allow him to fulfil the hopes that had been held out to the Irish Roman Catholics before the Union, and he consequently gave up his office, but unwillingly and under pressure from Grenville and his other colleagues. The King, who knew that he and his family owed the throne to the desire of the English people to be protected against Roman Catholicism, was strongly opposed to any relaxation of the existing disabilities. He once stated in reference to his Coronation Oath, which required him to maintain the 'Protestant reformed religion, "Was not my family seated on the throne for that express purpose, and shall I be the first to suffer it to be undermined, perhaps overturned? No! I had rather beg my bread from door to door throughout Europe than consent to any such measure." On another occasion, after having read his Coronation Oath to his family, and enquired of them if they understood it, the King exclaimed, "If I violate it, I am no longer legal Sovereign of this country, but it falls to the House of Savoy."

Dundas told Sir James Mackintosh that, at the time of the Union with Ireland, he had a conversation with the King on the subject of a proposal for the relief of the Catholics. "I hope," said the King, "Government is not pledged to anything in favour of the Romanists." "No," answered Dundas, "but it will be a matter for future consideration whether, to render the measure the more efficient, it will not be proper to embrace them in some liberal plan of policy." "What say you to my Coronation Oath?" asked the King. "That can only apply to your majesty, I conceive, in your executive capacity. It does not refer to you as part of the legislature." "None of your Scotch metaphysics, Mr Dundas," replied the King. On another occasion in January, 1801, the King walked up to Dundas at a levée, and eagerly asked him, referring to Lord Castlereagh, and the proposals for the relief of the Catholics, "What is it that this young Lord has brought over which they are going to throw at my head?...the most Jacobinical thing I ever heard of! I shall reckon any man my personal enemy who proposes any such measure." "Your majesty," said Dundas, "will find among those who are friendly to that measure some whom you never supposed to be your enemies." Dundas himself assigned the King's attitude as the cause of Pitt's resignation. He said to Mackintosh that, from his experience in affairs, he had been taught to have very little faith in historians. "For instance," he stated, "the motives I and my colleagues have assigned for our resignation, drawn from the popery question, no historian will believe; and, if any mentions it, he will treat it as a mere pretext to cover the real motive; and he will support his representation by very plausible arguments; yet nothing can be more true than that the reason we assigned was the real one. The King was prepared to oppose us on the popery question."

CHAPTER VIII

Dundas retired with his chief, and resigned the Secretaryship of State. His resignation, after a reign so long and unquestioned, naturally created a great sensation in Scotland. Brougham has described, in amusing terms, the universal dismay and the doubts as to what would follow. The public mind in Scotland, he says, was subdued with awe, and men awaited in trembling silence the uncertain event, as all living things quail during the solemn pause which precedes an earthquake. All was uncertainty and consternation. No man could tell whom he might trust. Nay, says Brougham, no man could tell of whom he might ask anything.

"But such a crisis," he continues, "was too sharp to last; it passed away; and then was to be seen a proof of Mr Dundas's power amongst his countrymen, which transcended all expectation, and almost surpassed belief, if indeed it is not rather to be viewed as an evidence of the acute foresight—the political second-sight—of the Scottish nation. The trusty band in both Houses actually were found adhering to him against the existing Government; nay, though in opposition, he held the proxies of many Scottish peers! Well might his colleague exclaim to the hapless Addington, in such unheard-of troubles, ' Doctor[1], the Thanes fly from us!'"

On 1st October, 1801, the Addington ministry agreed to the preliminaries of peace with France. Ceylon and

---

[1] "Doctor" was a nickname fastened by Canning on Addington, whose father had been physician to Chatham.

Trinidad were to be retained. The Cape of Good Hope was to be restored to the Dutch and made a free port. Malta was to be given back to the Order of the Knights of St John. Egypt was to be returned to the Turks. The kingdom of Naples and the Roman territory were to be evacuated by the French. Pitt approved the treaty, describing it as "highly honourable and advantageous to the country, although not perhaps in every point exactly all that was to be wished." Grenville, on the other hand, was intensely indignant, and especially at the surrender of the Cape and Malta. He strenuously opposed the treaty in Parliament, and when the definite Peace was signed at Amiens in March, 1802, fiercely denounced it. But public opinion was almost unanimously in favour of the treaty, and his protests had little effect. Grenville, however, would not forgive the ministry, and henceforth assailed it with intense hostility.

In his first disgust with the terms of the treaty, Grenville had written to Pitt and Dundas for their opinion upon them. Pitt had defended the Peace as highly expedient in existing circumstances. Dundas had written a diplomatic letter marked *Private and Confidential*, in which he emphatically condemned the concessions to France, but declared his intention to refrain from all censure, private as well as public, so as not to weaken an administration acceptable to the King. He added that it was not impossible that he might retire altogether from Parliament. He found himself, he said, so comfortable with his farm and his plantations, that it would require very little additional inducement to persuade him to make his retirement from all public business perfectly complete. From this letter it is evident that Dundas wished to stand well with Addington, if indeed he was not in confidential relations with him. When Grenville attacked the treaty in Parliament, Dundas went out of his way to sneer at the "new opposition,"—the name given to the Grenville Party—as a factious clique. By doing so he terminated the more or less friendly connexion which had existed for twenty years between Grenville and himself. At the General Election in the summer of 1802 Dundas further showed his friendliness to Addington by consenting to manage the Scottish constituencies on behalf of the ministers, and did so with such success that only two of the forty-five members returned were Whigs. The result of his assistance to Addington was his elevation in December to the peerage as Viscount Melville of Melville in the county of Edinburgh, and Baron Dunira of Dunira in the county of Perth. Dundas had fallen out of touch with Pitt, and the latter was greatly surprised when he heard the news. "I have not," said Pitt, "heard one syllable from him on the subject since we parted in the summer; indeed, I have had no letter from him for some months. But what is most extraordinary, Dundas, when I last saw him, stated to me a variety of reasons why it was impossible for him to accept a peerage."

In March, 1803, Lord Melville, as Dundas must now be called, took a step which still further showed his friendliness to Addington. At Addington's request, he conveyed a message to Pitt, asking him to take office in the administration. It is difficult to say what were the Prime Minister's motives in approaching Pitt. Addington may have been actuated by a growing sense of the weakness of his position, or he may have been influenced by a desire to prevent Pitt from taking up a decidedly hostile position to his government, and exposing his financial miscalculations. The proposal was that Addington should resign the Premiership and become a Secretary of State, and that Pitt should also become a Secretary of State, or, if he preferred it, Chancellor of the Exchequer, while a third person was to be the nominal head of the administration. Pitt's brother, Lord Chatham, was suggested as a person likely to be acceptable to Pitt. Lord St Vincent, who was a singularly inefficient First Lord of the Admiralty, was to make way for Melville. Pitt was staying at Walmer Castle, his official residence as Warden of the Cinque Ports, when Melville arrived there on Sunday morning, 20th March, as ambassador from Addington. In the evening after dinner, as they sat at the table lighted up by the tall candles, and bearing the inevitable decanters of port, Melville cautiously revealed his message to Pitt. He had not gone very far in his explanations when he realised that his task was a vain one. To a statesman, whose motto had ever been *Aut Caesar aut nihil,* and who had ruled the Empire for seventeen years, the proposals of Addington must have seemed somewhat astonishing. Some weeks later Pitt related the incident to Wilberforce, who in after years used to describe it to his friends. Melville, says Wilberforce, saw it would not do, and stopped abruptly. "'Really,' said Pitt, with a sly severity—and it was almost the only sharp thing," says Wilberforce, "I ever heard him say of any friend—'I had not the curiosity to ask what I was to be.'" But although the conversation might have been cut short on the first evening Pitt did not refuse to hear, and to consider the proposals of Melville next day. He met them, however, with an unhesitating negative, and in the end the negotiations came to nothing.

As time went on, the position of Addington became more and more difficult. In May, 1803, war was again

declared upon France, but the preparations made by
the government were wholly inadequate. The criminal
supineness of the ministry convinced Pitt that he must
once more pilot the State. He made a vigorous attack
on the imbecility and tardiness of the administration in
the House of Commons, and on 10th May, 1804, Addington
handed the seals of office to the King. They were given
by the King to Pitt, who at once accepted them, and
endeavoured to found a strong and united ministry,
which should include Fox and Grenville. The King
obstinately refused to accept Fox, who, with undoubted
generosity, submitted to the royal veto, and advised
Grenville and his own friends to support the ministry.
Grenville, however, refused to serve with Pitt, making
the exclusion of Fox his excuse for so acting. Pitt
greatly resented the conduct of his kinsman and former
colleague, in refusing to help him in a crisis of national
difficulty. He would teach that proud man, he told Lord
Eldon, that, in the service of, and with the confidence of
his sovereign, he would do without him, even though the
effort might cost him his life. Lord Malmesbury, in
commenting upon Grenville's conduct in his Diary, not
inaptly quoted the French proverb, "Un bon ami vaut
mieux que trois mauvais parents."

On 15th May Melville was appointed First Lord of the
Admiralty. His predecessor, Lord St Vincent, though a
victorious admiral, had been an incompetent administrator,
and Melville found things appertaining to the Navy in a
highly unsatisfactory condition. He discovered that there
were only eighty-one ships of the line available for service,
a number which he did not regard as sufficient. He devoted
himself to the work of increasing the navy with prompt
and vigorous energy, and his business capacities never

proved more useful. He gave large orders to the merchants' yards; he placed the King's yards on an efficient footing; he bought up in all directions materials of every kind, from timber down to hemp, for even hemp was wanting. He so stimulated the activity of the builders that he was able to say, when he addressed the House of Lords in May, 1805, that the whole force, either actually added to the navy or in a state of forwardness, appeared to amount to one hundred and sixty-eight vessels more than there were on the day of his accession to the office of First Lord of the Admiralty.

CHAPTER IX

There is a curious book of Scottish biography, written in the seventeenth century, which bears the quaint title of *The Staggering State of Scots Statesmen*. It is the work of Sir John Scot of Scotstarvet, and it describes the careers of the men who held the offices of State in Scotland between 1550 and 1650. The writer shows how many of those, who had been prominent in their day, had suffered at the hands of capricious Fortune. Some of them attained great power, and lost it. Some were great till death, but always had to endure some fly in the ointment or some skeleton in the closet. Some, who built up the prosperity of their houses on what appeared to be sure foundations, had sons or grandsons, who came to the dust. The reader realises the instability of Fortune, when he reads, for example, how John Stuart, who became Lord Treasurer of Scotland and Earl of Traquair, was so reduced in the end that he had to beg alms in the open streets of Edinburgh. As Lucan says,

> "Sic longius aevum
> Destruit ingentis animos et vila superstes
> Imperio."

The Staggering State of Scots Statesmen was to be strikingly exemplified in the career of Lord Melville. After long years of authority, he fell from power in the most dramatic fashion in 1805. In 1785 Melville had carried an Act for "better regulating the office of Treasurer of the Navy," with the object of preventing the Treasurer from appropriating any part of the money, passing through his hands, to his own private use. The lucrative perquisites attaching to his office were abolished, but the salary was raised from £2000 to £4000 with allowances, which made the remuneration in all little short of £5000. It was alleged, however, that, in spite of this Act, malversation and corruption still continued to exist in the navy civil departments, and, when Lord St Vincent was at the head of the Admiralty, five Commissioners were appointed to enquire into the frauds and irregularities, which were believed to be going on. The Commissioners issued twelve reports and a supplementary one. The tenth report, which dealt with the office of Treasurer of the Navy, was understood, even before it was made public, to reflect upon the conduct of Melville, while holding that office. Everybody was eagerly looking for the publication of the document, and nobody more anxiously than Pitt. As it happened Wilberforce was calling on him at his office on the same morning that the first copy was brought in. "I shall never forget," says Wilberforce, "the way in which he seized it, and how eagerly he looked into the leaves without waiting even to cut them open."

Great excitement was aroused in political and commercial circles by the publication of the Tenth Report. It clearly showed that Alexander Trotter, who had been appointed Paymaster of the Navy by Melville, had misapplied the public money. Sums derived from the revenue had been paid to his own account with Coutts, his private bankers, and used in his private speculations. Trotter defended himself before the Commissioners by urging that the public had not sustained any loss by his use of public money, but the Commissioners refused to allow any weight to his statements. The Commissioners examined Melville in person, and asked him whether he had advanced any of the money applicable to naval services for any other public service than that of the Navy. This question Melville declined to answer, pleading the fifth clause of the Act appointing the Commissioners, by which no man was obliged to criminate himself. A second question was then put, "Did Trotter ever lay out any public money for your private advantage?" Melville's answer was that from the way in which the accounts were kept by Trotter, it was impossible to answer the question. But he wrote a letter in June, 1804, to the Commissioners in which he reminded them that, while Treasurer of the Navy, he had held other confidential positions. So situated, he said, he did not decline giving occasional accommodation from the funds in the Treasurer's hands to other services not connected with his official situation as Treasurer of the Navy. Trotter, when examined, was so cautious that very little information was obtained from him, and Melville absolutely declined to tell the Commissioners for what purposes he had accommodated other services, on the ground that he could not do so without disclosing delicate and confidential transactions of government. Melville also stated in a letter to the Commissioners in March, 1805, that, to the best of his recollection, he had never derived any benefit or advantage from the money set apart for the current service of the Navy, and he added that there never was any arrangement between himself and Trotter that he should derive any such benefit or advantage, and that he never knowingly did so. He also said in the same letter that all sums lent to other services had been repaid, and that he had derived no private emolument from them.

The forces of the Opposition saw an excellent chance of striking at Pitt through his colleague, and they assailed Melville with a mighty show of righteous anger. The attack was led by Samuel Whitbread, the son of a self-made brewer, of Nonconformist descent and humble connexions. He had been the friend of Charles Grey, afterwards second Earl Grey, at Eton, and had married his sister. Loud, vulgar, and unrestrained by any require-ments of good taste, he threw himself into his task with zeal and gusto. The opponents of the administration refused to believe the statement of Melville as to advances for Secret Service, and alleged that he had not hesitated to use those sums of money, or, at all events, the interest from them, for his private use and profit. Much stress was laid upon the persistence with which he had clung to the office of Treasurer of the Navy, at which even Pitt, according to Addington, had expressed surprise. Whitbread pointed out that, although Melville had added office to office, and frequently complained in the House of Commons of the amount of work which he had to do, yet he never resigned the post of Treasurer of the Navy. Wilberforce says that, some years before the issue of the Tenth Report, Thomas Raikes, the Governor of the Bank of England, had hinted to Pitt that the public money was illegally used. Melville came in soon after, and Pitt said to him, "Dundas, here has been Tom Raikes to me with a long story of your way of employing the public money. What does he mean?" Melville, says Wilberforce, assured him that it was their mistake, and that no money had been drawn except for public purposes.

Bitter Whigs, like Francis Horner, exulted in the slur

cast upon Pitt by the publication of the report. "The *historical* effect of the Tenth Report," he wrote to Dugald Stewart, "is decisively secured, and a long shade is thrown back upon the former ministry of Pitt." Even the King himself, who had never liked Melville, was said to have been secretly pleased at the discredit which he had incurred. It was stated that he asked every one, "Have you seen the Tenth Report? the Tenth Report?" It was alleged that the market had been affected by the dealings of Melville. "By God, sir," said the egregious Alderman Curtis, "we felt him in our market." The populace took up the lead given to them by their betters, and joined in hunting Melville down. The cry, wrote Horner to Mackintosh, was loud against Placemen and Scotsmen. A drama was being played in London at the time, called *The Wheel of Fortune*, in which an old Governor is represented as saying that he cannot give his daughter a portion, for he had never understood the arts of governing. The remark was received with uproarious applause, which even the presence of the King was powerless to suppress.

It was not only among the mob that Melville was unpopular. There is no doubt that his line of action since the resignation of Pitt in 1801 had laid him open to the enmity of many prominent persons in the political world. He had accepted a peerage from Addington, and yet deserted him on a vote of want of confidence, a proceeding which made him specially obnoxious to Addington's adherents. When Grenville translated into action opinions, in which Melville had privately concurred, and opposed the administration of Addington, Melville had made an unprovoked attack upon Grenville, and given indelible offence to old colleagues, who were united with

Grenville. Although Grenville abstained and advised others to abstain from countenancing the proceedings in Parliament against Melville, it did not lessen the un-seemliness of Melville's conduct. Grenville might justly write, as he did to Lord Wellesley in October, 1806, "I must say that, if there be one individual in this country to whom I conceive myself to have shown the *greatest* kindness, and that too with much embarrassment and difficulty, that individual is Lord Melville."

After the publication of the Report, Whitbread gave notice, through his brother-in-law, Grey, that on the 8th of April he would bring the contents of it before the House of Commons. The slippery sycophants of power at once began to desert Melville. The sneaking crowd of flatterers fell rapidly away.

> "We worldly men, when we see friends and kinsmen
> Past hope sunk in their fortunes, lend no hand
> To lift them up, but rather set our feet
> Upon their heads to press them to the bottom."

Addington, who had now become Lord Sidmouth, thought the evidence in the report conclusive, and proposed that Melville should at once resign, without waiting to be attacked. Pitt, however, was from the first staunchly loyal to his colleague, and determined to defend him. He refused to listen to the suggestions of Wilberforce and others of his friends, that he should abandon him. Many even of his opponents admired his loyalty to Melville, and Lord Holland thought his conduct in standing by his colleague the most amiable passage of his life. Wilber-force said long afterwards that Pitt was led into supporting Melville chiefly by "that false principle of honour, which was his great fault." But it was not primarily from a sense of honour that Pitt defended Melville. He knew the nature of the man, and believed him, although culpably lax in his superintendence of Trotter's accounts, to be innocent of all personal corruption. Melville was as indifferent to mere wealth as Disraeli was, and Pitt believed, as he told Wilberforce, that there had been no real pocketing of public money.

On 8th April Whitbread moved a series of eleven resolutions condemning in the strongest terms the conduct of Melville. The Cabinet, on the other hand, as a counter-proposal, asked the House to agree to the appointment of a Select Committee of enquiry. The Prime Minister tried to show that, in justice to the accused person, each charge required further investigation, and that this ought to be made by a Select Committee before the House was called upon to give its decision. On the other side Fox exerted all his powers against Melville, from whom he had always had an aversion. As one would expect, he was bitter and malignant.

"It has been said," he declared, "that the House should proceed with the utmost deliberation in deciding upon character. But upon whose character were they to decide on this occasion. Not, certainly, upon that of Lord Melville, for his character was entirely gone; but upon the character of the House and the Government, which must depend upon the vote of this night. As to the character of Lord Melville, it was so completely destroyed in public estimation for ever, that he would venture to say, that, were the vote of the House unanimous in his favour, it would not have the slightest effect in wiping away the stigma that was universally affixed to his name."

And later on he continues in still stronger language,

"Really, Sir, I have a strong repugnance to enter into all the disgusting particulars of the conduct of this person with whom I had once some slight connection. God knows, it was a connection of hostility; but after what appears on the face of this report, I should be ashamed of myself, if I belonged to the same class of society with him.''

In the divided state of the House the opinion of Wilberforce was looked to with eager interest. The independent members had learnt from Pitt himself to attach great importance to purity and scrupulous integrity where public money was concerned, and they looked forward with curiosity to the decision of Wilberforce, whose high character commanded universal respect. When he rose late at night, after waiting until almost the last to hear and weigh all the arguments, a thrill of expectation was felt. He sat at the end of the Treasury bench, and he related long afterwards that, when he rose and turned towards the Speaker, he looked just across Pitt, and observed him listen with intense eagerness for the first intimation of the course which he was going to take. "It required no little effort," said Wilberforce, "to resist the fascination of that penetrating eye." But he soon made it clear what view he took. He gave, he said, his most cordial and sincere support to Whitbread's motion. He was strongly impressed, he said, with the culpable conduct of Melville, and could not refuse to satisfy the moral sense of the country.

The House divided upon the motion at four o'clock in the morning in breathless silence, and the numbers were found to be exactly equal. There were 216 for the motion, and the same number against it. It thus fell to the Speaker to give the casting vote. He became as pale as a sheet, and, after pausing for some minutes, gave his vote against Melville. Lord Fitzharris, who was then one of the Treasury Board, and afterwards became the second Earl of Malmesbury, was sitting wedged close to Pitt

himself, when the division was taken.   He states that the
following incident took place.

"Pitt immediately put on the little cocked hat that he was
in the habit of wearing when dressed for the evening, and
jammed it deeply over his forehead, and I distinctly saw the
tears trickling down his cheeks.   We had overheard one or
two, such as Colonel Wardle (of notorious memory) say they
would see 'how Billy looked after it.'   A few young ardent
followers of Pitt, with myself, locked their arms together and
formed a circle, in which he moved, I believe unconsciously,
out of the House; and neither the Colonel nor his friends could
approach him."

One is sorry to question the truth of an oft-quoted
anecdote, which is inseparably associated with the
memory of Pitt.   There are good reasons, however, for
believing that it has no foundation in fact.   Pitt could
not have gone out of the House immediately after the
division, because he moved an amendment, and spoke
three times after it took place.   He could not therefore
have been so moved; indeed he was on his legs when
strangers entered after the division.   As for Colonel
Wardle, he was not elected to the House of Commons
till June, 1807, and could not have been present at all.
The story, picturesque as it is, must be relegated to the
limbo of romance.

The Opposition hailed the carrying of the first resolution with tumultuous joy.   One red-coat squire, Sir
Thomas Mostyn, raised what he called a *view-hollo*, and
cried out, "We have killed the fox."   When the remaining
resolutions had been put and carried, Whitbread proposed
an address to the King, asking him to remove Melville
from his councils.   On the suggestion of Pitt, the consideration of this motion was postponed till the day but
one after, and the House then rose at half-past five in the

morning.   It is perhaps right to say that the King, Pitt, and Robert Dundas, the son of Melville, all agreed that the Speaker had acted properly in giving the casting vote as he did.   On the next day Melville resigned his office of First Lord of the Admiralty, and the post was given to his kinsman, Sir Charles Middleton, an octogenarian admiral, who was created Lord Barham.

CHAPTER X

After the Easter Recess the House again met, and on the very first night Whitbread rose to enquire whether Pitt intended to recommend the King to expunge the name of Melville from the list of the Privy Council. Pitt answered that he had no such intention. It seemed, he said, to be the sense of the House, when the affair was last discussed, that a removal from any place of trust and confidence would be sufficient, till further light was thrown upon the subject by the investigations of a Select Committee. Whitbread at once announced that he would raise the question of removal from the Privy Council on a future day, and then proceeded to move that the Tenth Report should be referred to a Select Committee. His proposal was, with some modifications, adopted, and on 30th April the Select Committee was appointed. The motion with reference to the removal of Melville from the Privy Council was fixed for 6th May. Pitt was warned that he would be defeated if he resisted the motion, but he was resolved to stand by his friend. The situation was relieved by Melville himself, who wrote to Pitt, practically consenting to the removal of his name. He concluded his letter by a pathetic allusion to the unremitting distress and agitation, which the debates, so full of personal asperity, produced in his family circle. Accordingly, when the matter was brought before the

House by Whitbread, Pitt said that he had advised the
King to erase the name of Melville from the list of Privy
Councillors, and that the erasure would take place on the
first day that a Council was held. He concluded with the
words, "I confess, Sir, and I am not ashamed to confess
it, that whatever may be my deference to the House of
Commons, and however anxious I may be to accede to
their wishes, I certainly felt a deep and bitter pang in
being compelled to be the instrument of rendering still
more severe the punishment of the Noble Lord." Lord
Macaulay, who had heard accounts of the scene from
several persons who were present, has described it in
vivid terms. As Pitt uttered the word 'pang,' says
Macaulay, his lip quivered; his voice shook; he paused;
and his hearers thought that he was about to burst into
tears. He suppressed his emotion, however, and proceeded with his usual majestic self-possession.

The Committee on the Tenth Report presented their
report to the House towards the end of May. It was
unfavourable to the accused statesman, and dwelt
especially on two sums, amounting together to upwards
of £20,000, which it was acknowledged that Melville had
received as Treasurer of the Navy, and had applied to
other than naval purposes. As Whitbread was threatening
another attack, Melville asked permission to address the
House of Commons in his own defence and, the permission
having been obtained, he appeared before the House on
the 11th of June. A chair for his reception having been
placed within the Bar, he took his seat and covered
himself. In a few minutes he took off his hat, rose, and
began to address the House. The sight must have been
an affecting one. To Fox, fresh from gambling hells, and
Whitbread, fresh from his mash-tubs, it was no doubt

gratifying to see their old opponent sitting as a culprit at the Bar. But to men whose souls had not been blackened by the bitter party spirit of the eighteenth century, and who retained any sentiment of kindliness, the spectacle must have been painful and pathetic. Well might Melville say, "This is not such a conclusion as I had hoped for, and as I think I had a right to expect, to a long and laborious life devoted to my country's service."

Melville, who spoke for two hours and twenty minutes, denied that he had ever authorised Trotter, his paymaster, to take public money from the bank, and invest it in exchequer bills, or lend it on the security of stocks, or use it in discounting private bills or in buying India stock. He explained that Trotter, while in a subordinate position, attracted his notice by his zeal in pointing out the means, which were used to deprive seamen and their families of the full amount of what they were justly entitled to, and that, on the death of the paymaster, he had promoted him to the vacant post. He gave an instance of his own sturdy courage when he declared that, whatever anxiety Trotter might have caused him, he had to acknowledge that that official had conducted the pay office of the Navy for fourteen years without a moment's delay in any payment at the Treasurer's office, and an account of not less than one hundred and thirty-four million pounds sterling had been closed without the loss of one farthing to the public during the whole of that period. He finished a long speech in tones of becoming dignity and conscious innocence.

"I trust," he said, "that nothing in the course of this day has fallen from me in any degree disrespectful to the assembly which with their indulgence I have been permitted to address;

but I equally trust I cannot be liable to censure if I have not in any part of what I have said shown a disposition to deprecate, by humiliating submission, any of the future evils which may be in contemplation against me."

His concluding words were :

"I despair not, even in my own time, to receive ample justice from my deluded country....I feel the consciousness of my own rectitude deeply implanted in my breast, and I shall descend to my grave with the heartfelt satisfaction that, however the shafts of severity and cruelty may be levelled against me at the present moment, the future impartial historian will be able to hand down my name in the list of those who have strenuously, and, I hope, not ineffectually exerted, during a long life of public service, their unremitting endeavours to promote the welfare and the dearest and most essential interests of their country."

The speech of Melville did not prevent the House of Commons from resolving that he should be impeached. His tone was considered too haughty and defiant, and it was freely said that his defence had injured instead of helping his cause. The truth was that his enemies wanted to see him bowed down to the dust, and were annoyed because he showed no inclination to make a humiliating submission. In considering the charges against him, the House was performing a judicial function, and should have preserved a judicial spirit. The Opposition, however, seemed rather to regard themselves as hunters with Melville as the fox, and pursued and hounded him with savage bitterness. The view-hollo of Sir Thomas Mostyn, which has been already referred to, was a striking indication of the spirit which actuated Whitbread and his gang. When Lord Henley walked into Brooke's Club on the day after the resolutions had passed the House of Commons, he found the members, as he writes to Lord Auckland, "ivres de joie." Lord Malmesbury said that the transactions relating to Melville exceeded in party spirit and savage feeling all that he ever recollected in this country. What, he asks, would these very men have said to the judges and jury, had they behaved thus at the sentence of the most bloodthirsty felon[1].

There were many who were disgusted by the venom and malignancy shown towards Melville, and who thought, with Cromwell in *King Henry VIII*,

> "'Tis a cruelty
> To load a falling man."

The same thing happened in the case of Melville as happened, according to Tacitus, in the case of Piso. *Miseratio quam invidia augebatur*; pity prevailed over ill-will. The King in particular was disgusted with the conduct of Melville's opponents. He had never liked Melville[2]. He told George Rose in 1804 that he had never had any confidence in Melville, nor any friendship for him. Bland Burges says that the King was repelled by the laxity of Melville's private life, by his forward and familiar manner and his broad Scots dialect, and above all by his handwriting which, according to Burges, the King declared to be the worst and most ungentle-manlike he had ever met with. It is consequently not

---

[1] It is interesting to note that Napoleon was keenly watching what was going on in England, and was not long in turning Melville's disgrace to good account. "Faites faire," he wrote to Barbé Marbois on 2nd May, 1805, "un petit pamphlet sur l'affaire Melville pour montrer l'immoralité de M. Pitt et du gouvernement Anglais. Un écrit bien frappé la rendra évidente à tout le monde, et l'immoralité des chefs n'est point indifférente pour leur crédit."

[2] In his introduction to the seventh volume of the *Dropmore Papers*, Mr Fitzpatrick says that Melville was "a favourite at court." It was not so.

surprising that at first George manifested but little sympathy for the fallen minister. The Duke of Clarence told Lord Colchester in after years that, when informed about his arraignment by the House of Commons, he remarked, "Is that all? I wonder how he slept after it. Bring my horse." One may be pardoned for doubting the truth of this story, but, whether it be true or not, the King became disgusted, as he observed the continued and persistent malignity of Whitbread and his friends. In May he wrote to Pitt that he was much hurt at the virulence against Melville, "which is unbecoming the character of Englishmen, who naturally, when a man is fallen, are too noble to pursue their blows." And again in June he wrote objecting to any further measures being taken against him. "All that is necessary for example to futurity has been done," said the King, "and anything more is a wanton punishing of a fallen man, which is not the usual conduct of an Englishman, who never strikes his enemy when at his feet."

The feeling of disgust that was shown by the King was expressed by the caricaturists in another way. A picture by Gillray in July, 1805, represents Melville as "The Wounded Lion," extended helplessly on his side, while some jackasses are preparing to assail him. Two of the jackasses purport to represent Hiley Addington, the brother of Sidmouth, and Bragge Bathurst, his brother-in-law. One is made to say to the other, "Very highly indebted to the lion, brother Hiley," and the answer is, "Then kick him again, brother Bragge." In another caricature by Sayer, entitled "The Brewer and the Thistle," Whitbread, a figure built up of tubs and barrels, is represented as aiming a blow at Melville, the Scottish thistle, with his flail. Underneath are the lines,

"Sansterre forsook his malt and grains,
To mash and batter nobles' brains,
By levelling rancour led;
Our Brewer quits brown stout and washey,
His malt, his mash-tub, and his quashea,
To mash a thistle's head."

After the impeachment of Melville had been decided on, but before it was commenced, the noble spirit of William Pitt had passed away. In December, 1805, Pitt and Melville had their last interview at Bath. The two old friends never met again. "When Mr Pitt at Bath showed me the distribution of the fleet," wrote Melville to Castlereagh, "I pointed out to him the deficiency; he told me he would have it remedied the moment he went to town—but alas!" Melville was profoundly affected by the death of his leader. The young Lord Aberdeen, who was himself afterwards to be Prime Minister, had lived much with Pitt and Melville, who were his guardians, or, as the Scottish legal phrase is, curators. Writing in his diary of Melville's sorrow at the time, he said that he never witnessed grief more poignant, and in a letter to a friend on the same day he stated that Melville was in absolute despair.

The death of Pitt, enfeebled in health and haunted by anxiety, is said by Lord Malmesbury and other contemporary writers, to have been hastened by the fall of Melville. "Some," says Lord Rosebery, adopting their view, "have ascribed his death to Ulm, and some to Austerlitz; but if the mortal wound was triple, the first stab was the fall of Dundas." It may be doubted, however, whether Pitt's concern for Dundas has not been exaggerated. Before his resignation in 1801, Pitt had ceased to regard Melville with the same cordiality as in earlier days. He had been seriously annoyed and probably alienated by Melville's dealings with Sidmouth. When Melville received his peerage, Pitt said he had not had a letter from Dundas for some months, which certainly does not suggest an intimate degree of friendship. Sir George Rose relates that, in a conversation with George the Third about Melville towards the end of 1804, the King said that he had reason to think that Melville did not then possess the same influence over Pitt as he formerly did. He told Rose, as a proof of it, that Melville, on his first seeing him, after it was agreed that he should be at the head of the Admiralty, told the King that he should like to know the particulars of what had passed with Pitt, as he had seen very little of him. This, said the King, surprised him somewhat, but he had thereupon related to Melville the whole of what had occurred. When the Tenth Report was published, Wilberforce, whose opportunities for knowing the real state of affairs were very great, said that, while it was generally thought that Pitt defended Melville out of friendship, he knew they were scarcely upon speaking terms. Wilberforce did not think that Pitt's health had been affected by the proceedings against Melville. Probably the truth is that Pitt's anxiety to clear Melville was not so much for Melville's sake as for the reputation of his own ministry. Horner's comments, already quoted, show that the Tenth Report was regarded as throwing a slur upon Pitt himself. It is true that Pitt said to Huskisson at Bath, "We can get over Auster-litz, but we can never get over the Tenth Report." But Pitt was probably thinking of the effect of the report not on Melville's character, but on his own administration. The incident, in which Colonel Wardle was alleged to figure, and which is usually cited to prove his concern for Melville, is obviously mythical, and Pitt's emotion, when he announced the removal of Melville's name from the list of Privy Councillors, cannot be too much relied on, as evidence of attachment to Melville, in face of other and contradictory circumstances.

The impeachment of Melville was commenced in Westminster Hall on 29th April, 1806. The event excited the greatest interest, and the scene was one of imposing splendour. "I never knew," the future Lord Chancellor Campbell wrote to his father, "what earthly magnificence was till yesterday, when I was present at Lord Melville's trial. Ye gods! the peeresses' box! A glory seemed to play round their countenances, and to shoot in vivid flashes to the extremities of the Hall." Whitbread opened the case for the prosecution, and both Piggott, the Attorney-General, and Romilly, the Solicitor-General, were heard on behalf of the Commons during the course of the proceedings. Melville was defended by Plomer, who was afterwards Master of the Rolls, Adam, and Hobhouse. Whitbread declaimed in a velvet coat, a bag wig, and laced ruffles. Charles Kirkpatrick Sharpe, the anti-quarian, who was present, wrote a description of the scene to a friend.

"You would have laughed, had you seen the ridiculous care with which his (Whitbread's) friends gave him sips of wine and water to wet his whistle, and clouts for his mouth and nose. I thought his speech very clever but in a miserable bad taste, and so abusive that Lord Melville smiled very frequently. That monster Fox was there, his sallow cheeks hanging down to his paunch, and his scowling eyes turned sometimes upon Mr Whitbread, sometimes on the rows of pretty peeresses who sat eating sandwiches from silk indis-pensables, and putting themselves into proper attitudes to astonish the representatives of the Commons of England, occupying the opposite benches."

Whitbread displayed prodigious diligence in preparing the case, and in mastering the transactions which he had to explain. It was said, however, that he was too anxious to display his own wit and eloquence, and too much occupied, as the Duchess of Gordon expressed it, in teaching "his dray-horse to caper," with the result that he failed to convince. It may be that Whitbread lessened the effect of his oratory by faults of manner and style, but, after a careful perusal of the speeches, the present writer is not disposed to join unreservedly in the contemporary condemnation. The final effort of Whitbread seems to him a powerful and able oration. Whitbread took the management of the case into his own hands, and insisted on his own methods in opposition to the general views of the managers and of his friend Romilly in particular. He offered himself as a witness to prove the substance of Melville's defence in the House of Commons, and the counsel for the accused man took advantage of Whitbread's position—with a spice of malicious pleasure, perhaps—to subject him to a long and severe cross-examination. Whitbread bitterly resented the action of Melville's counsel, and complained that it in no degree tended to "soften the asperity of dissertation." He had intended to call the Speaker to give evidence, but he said that he could not expose the dignity of the House of Commons, after the rude cross-examination which he himself had experienced.

On the conclusion of the proceedings in Westminster Hall the peers discussed the evidence with closed doors, and certain questions were submitted to the Judges. On 12th June the House of Lords re-assembled, and acquitted Melville on all the charges. The majorities in his favour varied from twenty-seven to one hundred and twenty-eight, while on the fourth charge the acquittal was unanimous. On the second and third charges, which were the strongest items in the case for the prosecution, and which accused Melville of permitting Trotter, his paymaster, to withdraw public money from the Bank of England, and of conniving at its use by Trotter for his own private emolument, Melville was only acquitted by majorities of twenty-seven and thirty-one. Lord Erskine, the Lord Chancellor, presided over the proceedings before the peers with singular fairness. The Hastings trial, which had lasted over many years, had brought the process of impeachment into great disrepute, but Erskine took care that no discredit should be thrown upon his conduct of Melville's trial. During the fifteen days covered by the proceedings, his demeanour on the woolsack, says Lord Campbell, excited universal admiration for dignity, for courtesy, for impartiality, for firmness, and for discrimination. The bearing of Melville himself was all that it ought to have been. Mrs Charlotte Nugent attended the trial every day, and, writing to Admiral Cornwallis, she said that Lord Melville's conduct was highly dignified, and that no man's in such a predicament could be more so. He was, she said, steady and respectful to the House, actively employed with his counsel, and betraying no marks of anger or want of patience at the most severe language. She added that his situation put her in mind of Cardinal Wolsey. Other spectators write less complacently. "The scene is horrid," wrote Sir Gilbert Elliot. "Lord Melville looks like death. I never saw anybody more terribly altered."

CHAPTER XI

The acquittal of Melville excited the indignation of the more bitter among the Whigs. Lord Holland thought the trial had been miserably managed by the Commons. He writes of the conduct of the peers in his usual ill-natured and venomous way. He speaks of Lord Erskine's ignorance of forms, and Lord Ellenborough's intemperance. He points out that Lord Grenville and Lord Spencer absented themselves after the third day of the trial, and alleges that the questions which they asked and the period at which they retired from the investigation, were thought to imply an unwillingness to convict, almost equivalent to a disposition to screen, their old colleague. Lord Eldon, says Lord Holland, acknowledged, in addressing the House, that he would rather cut off his right arm than be guilty of such "culpable negligence" and "criminal indulgence" as Melville, but he defended him on technical arguments, on which he procured a reference to the Judges. Francis Horner, a bigoted Whig, was deeply depressed by the verdict, which he regarded as contrary to plain strong accumulated evidence. Writing to his friend, Murray, he said that he considered the acquittal as a foul stain upon the records of parliamentary justice.

The substantial innocence of Melville was taken for granted after Party feeling had subsided. Whitbread himself, according to Yonge, the biographer of Lord

Liverpool, subsequently admitted that he had never suspected Melville of having personally enriched himself by these transactions. An excellent instance of the change effected by the dying down of personal enmity and the passage of time, which softens and mellows all things, is afforded by Brougham. Writing when the Whigs were in full cry after Melville, he speaks in the severest terms of Melville's conduct. "It is something," he says, "that such sharks should be brought to justice." And again he laments that Pitt should have been so long coupled "with such a nasty dog." In later life, however, when he wrote his chapter on Melville in his *Sketches of English Statesmen*, he vindicates him from the charge that had been brought against him. "The case proved against him," he says, "was not by any means so clear as to give us the right to charge the great majority of his peers with corrupt and dishonourable conduct in acquitting him; while it is a known fact that the Judges who attended the trial were, with the exception of the Lord Chief Justice, all clearly convinced ot his innocence."

While fully appreciating the allegations that Melville was innocent, the present writer will candidly confess that the impression left upon his mind, after reading the report of the trial, was not quite as favourable to Melville as he had expected it would be. There was a case to answer, and the matter was certainly one that required investigation. A minister, who had clung so tenaciously to the office of Treasurer of the Navy, who had destroyed all the papers throwing any light on the case against him, as soon as the Naval Commission was appointed, and who refused to answer questions on the ground that his replies would be prejudicial to the public interest, could not complain if an ill construction was put upon his conduct. The

strongest point in his favour was the comparative smallness of the sums which he is said to have used. During
the period in which Melville was employed as Treasurer
of the Navy one hundred and forty millions passed through
his hands. If he had been eager for money, he would, as
one of his counsel said, have dealt largely with the public
money. He would not have risked his reputation to pick
up minute sums of interest at a banker's. If he had been
disposed to peculate, as his Whig nephew, Lord Cockburn
said, it would not have been for farthings. Melville was
not a lover of money. He was, on the contrary, open-
handed, generous, and indifferent to wealth. After
holding the most dignified and lucrative situations in
the State, he remained a poor man, and left but a small
property at his death. Whitbread replied to the obser-
vation of Melville's counsel that the profuse generosity,
which Melville had always displayed, was incompatible
with the meanness attributed to him, by quoting Sallust's
description of Catiline. *Simulator ac dissimulator, alieni
appetens, sui profusus, satis eloquentiae, sapientiae parum.*
The quotation was a clever one, but it had no application
to Melville.

Not content, however, with putting forward the plea
that Melville was profuse and generous, his counsel made
the mistake of urging that his understanding was not
adapted to financial calculations. "He was never a man
disposed to figures," said Plomer, "to accounts, and to
minute arithmetical computations; he was never accustomed to them, perhaps unacquainted with them." This
plea, however, was a mistaken one, and soon broke down.
Whitbread refuted it by calling attention to the India
accounts, which Melville had periodically presented to
the House of Commons. "The prodigious complication

of those accounts," it was said, "rendered them dark and inscrutable even to men clear and luminous in their conception, until his lordship placed them in a point of view so distinct and methodical that he seemed to have devoted his whole life to arithmetical computation."

There is no doubt that Melville greatly injured his case by his support and adherence to his subordinate. There was no question that Trotter had been guilty of malversation, and was largely responsible for the position in which Melville was placed. Whitbread said that the guilt of Melville consisted only in his too great confidence and attachment to Trotter.

"Tantum infelicem nimium dilexit animum."

Trotter all along denied that Melville had had any knowledge of his speculations with the public money, or derived any benefit from them, and Melville generously reciprocated by placing his shield, as far as he could, over Trotter. He would have fared better, from a selfish point of view, if he had thrown over his servant.

It need hardly be said that the proceedings against Melville were followed with the utmost grief and dismay in Scotland. The champion, behind whose shield his friends and supporters had so long been sheltered, lay stricken on the ground. They might have asked the question Andrew Melville asked of Lord Glamis, the Chancellor of Scotland in the reign of James the Sixth,

"Tu, leo magne, jaces inglorius; ergo manebunt
Qualia fata canes?"

No one expressed a profounder sympathy with Melville than Walter Scott. "Poor Lord Melville! how does he look?" writes Scott to Ellis in February, 1806. "My heart bleeds when I think on his situation." And the poet quotes two lines from Smollett's *Tears of Scotland*,

"Even when the rage of battle ceased,
The victor's soul was not appeased."

Next month Scott again writes to Ellis,

"I own Lord Melville's misfortunes affect me deeply.... I have seen when the streets of Edinburgh were thought by the inhabitants almost too vulgar for Lord Melville to walk upon; and now I fear that, with his power and influence gone, his presence would be accounted by many, from whom he has deserved other thoughts, an embarrassment, if not something worse. All this is very vile—it is one of the occasions when Providence, as it were, industriously turns the tapestry, to let us see the ragged ends of the worsted which compose its most beautiful figures."

If the impeachment of Melville produced grief in Scotland, the dismissal of the charges against him caused the utmost delight. The joy of his friends and supporters was irrepressible, and excited the bitter chagrin of the Whigs. They had looked forward to the complete ruin of Melville. Dugald Stewart, for example, writing of the impeachment to Horner, said that he trusted it would close for ever the political career of Melville—"an event which I consider as synonymous with the emancipation and salvation of Scotland." An illumination was proposed in Edinburgh in honour of the acquittal. John Clerk, the Whig Solicitor-general, with singular meanness, tried to stop it. He wrote officially to the Lord Provost, saying that, if it took place, it would in his opinion lead to a popular outbreak for which the Lord Provost and the Town Council would be held responsible. An officer was sent through the town with tuck of drum, who read the letter and appealed to the public to repress the demonstration. This probably did not save a single candle, as

Cockburn said, but, as the illumination was partial, its shabbiness was ascribed plausibly enough to the illiberality of the Whigs.

A public dinner was given in honour of the acquittal on the 27th of June. It was for this dinner that Scott wrote the song, which was sung by James Ballantyne amidst clamorous applause, and which brought upon the writer a good deal of criticism. The song concluded

> "But the Brewer (Whitbread) we'll hoax,
> Tallyho to the Fox (Fox),
> And drink Melville for ever, as long as we live."

The words just quoted gave great offence to many of Scott's personal friends among the upper ranks of the Whigs; and he is said to have regretted them afterwards. But it is quite untrue to assert, as Walter Savage Landor did, that Scott "composed and sung a triumphal song on the death of a minister whom, in his lifetime, he had flattered, and who was just in his coffin when the minstrel sang *The Fox is run to Earth.*" This assertion is a tissue of falsehoods. The song was sung in June, 1806. Fox was then minister and did not die till September. Scott never used the words "the fox is run to earth," and the only lines in which Fox can be said to have been flattered by Scott were written, not during Fox's lifetime, but in the first canto of *Marmion*, published in February, 1808, nearly a year and a half after the death of the Whig leader.

Some of the lampoons and caricatures, which were published on Melville's acquittal were amusing. Whitbread in particular was a constant butt. He had shown great vanity and egotism in the course of the trial.

"My lords," he had said, "as long as your posterity shall represent this illustrious court of judicature; as long as the events of the country are transmitted to those descendants on the page of history; nay, even as long as the radiant orb of heaven expands his cheering beams over the earth, I trust, will the impeachment be carried down through revolving ages, and I glory in the reflection that my humble name will appear in the same annals, not on account of my personal merits, but from the blaze of that refulgence by which I am surrounded."

The vainglorious and extravagant language of Whitbread had been universally ridiculed. Canning had been so amused by some passages of his speech that he had scribbled a parody on them in rhyme, while Whitbread was yet speaking. The passage just quoted is thus rendered by Canning,

"So long as the beams of this house shall support
The roof which o'ershades this respectable court,
Where Hastings was tried for oppressing the Hindoos;
So long as that sun shall shine in at those windows,
My name shall shine bright as my ancestor's shines,
Mine recorded in journals, his blazoned on signs!"

A caricature by Rowlandson in July, 1806, entitled "The Acquittal or Upsetting the Porter Pot," represents Melville and Trotter in Highland garb, embracing each other. Melville is giving a backward kick at a huge pot, labelled "Whitbread's Entire Butt," and bearing Whitbread's face. Another caricature of Gillray in the same month, entitled "Bruin in his Boat or the Manager in Distress," represents Melville in kilt and tartan with thistles in his bonnet, standing on the "Rock of Innocence." He is firing off two guns, marked "Plomer," and "Adam[1]," with two torches, marked "Reason" and "Truth," into a ship entitled "the Impeachment," which has been wrecked near the "Rock of Honor." Another caricature of Gillray in July, 1806, represents Lord Chief Justice Ellenborough, sitting on a board marked "Broad Bottom

[1] The names of Melville's counsel.

Cabinet," and holding a pair of scales, in one of which is a roll marked "Impeachment," a pot of "Whitbread's Entire," and a "Sword of Justice." The other contains rolls bearing the words, "Decision of the Peers," "Opinion of the Eleven Judges," and other inscriptions, and is the heavier of the two.

Melville did not allow the impeachment to damp his interest in public affairs. Like Sallust, when he made up his mind to leave public affairs, "*non fuit consilium socordia atque desidia bonum otium conterere*," he had no mind to wear out his good leisure in listlessness and sloth. He was no sooner acquitted than he appeared in his place in the House of Lords to oppose the appointment of Lord Lauderdale to India, displaying thereby, in Lord Holland's opinion, "characteristic and constitutional effrontery." Although he never again held office, he soon recovered much of his old prestige. In the Scottish elections of 1806, he showed his old skill and success. On the formation of the Duke of Portland's ministry in 1807 a compliment was paid to him by the appointment of his eldest son as President of the Board of Control. On 8th April, 1807, Melville himself was restored to the Privy Council. When this was done Romilly said in the House of Commons that Ministers incurred a heavy responsibility in advising the King to summon to his councils a man, who, whenever he took his seat among the peers of England, must hear the words "guilty upon my honour" ringing in his ears. This rather fatuous remark was perhaps one of the "very foolish" expressions to which Romilly refers in his diary at this time. "My speech upon the whole was a very bad one, and was by no means favourably received by the House. I felt mortified and chagrined to the utmost degree....One or two expressions in my speech, which

I think were very foolish, have haunted my memory ever since I sat down."

The correspondence of Melville proves that, within a year after the termination of his trial, he was once more virtually the Minister for Scotland. Judging by the letters which were addressed to him by members of the Duke of Portland's ministry and by the public in Scotland, he had almost as much power from the year 1807 until his death as he had enjoyed when Pitt and he were paramount. In November, 1807, Lord Henry Petty wrote to Creevey that Melville was more than ever Minister *de facto* in Scotland, and that not a chaise was to be got on any of the roads which led to Dunira, his Highland home, so numerous were the solicitors and expectants that attended his court. In the previous April Melville himself had written to the wife of Lord President Blair, saying that, while he was happy in the enjoyment of quiet and repose and a tranquil mind, he had still the means of forwarding the wishes and interests of those who might have a claim on his attachment and friendship. In 1809 he received the offer of an earldom from Spencer Perceval, the Prime Minister, but declined it. There were rumours in the same year that he would return to office as First Lord of the Admiralty. Canning is said to have been most desirous that Melville should become a minister, and to have exclaimed against the political timidity of his colleagues who opposed it. Nothing, however, came of the suggestion, and on 14th June of the following year, 1810, Melville made his last speech in the House of Lords on the third reading of the Scotch Judicature Bill.

The end came in May, 1811. On the 20th of that month Robert Blair of Avontoun, the Lord President, died suddenly at his house, 56 George Square, Edinburgh, after a walk round Bruntsfield Links. Melville was greatly distressed at the death of one who was his kinsman and intimate friend, and came from Dunira to Edinburgh to attend the funeral. On Sunday, 25th, he went to Arniston with his daughter, Mrs Dundas, the wife of the Lord Chief Baron. On Tuesday, 27th, he returned to Edinburgh, where he dined and spent the evening with his son-in-law, the Lord Chief Baron, whose wife he had left at Arniston. He was saddened and depressed, and said that he dreaded the funeral of Blair, which was to take place the next day. He went to his room early, and spent some time alone writing letters. One letter was to Blair's widow, and another was to Perceval, recommending that a pension should be granted to Mrs Blair. Of the letter to Perceval Cockburn states, "It has always been said, and never, so far as I know, contradicted, and I am inclined to believe it, that a letter written by him was found on his table or in a writing case giving a feeling account of his emotions at the President's funeral." The sting of the story, if there is one, lies in the fact that the funeral had not then taken place. Oppressed by melancholy reflections, Melville retired to rest, and next morning, the 28th,—the anniversary of Pitt's birthday—he was found by his servant dead in bed. The residence of the Chief Baron was 57 George Square, next door to that of the Lord President, and so on the morning of the 28th the two old friends lay dead in adjoining houses with only the wall of partition between. Melville was buried in one of the aisles of the old church of Lasswade in Midlothian.

The death of Blair and Melville in the same week created a great impression. Sir Walter Scott wrote to his friend, Morritt, that Melville's death, so quickly succeeding that of President Blair, one of the best and wisest judges that ever distributed justice, had broken his spirit sadly. In a *Monody* by an anonymous writer, the characters of Melville and Blair were drawn with tolerable ability, and their friendship and death were celebrated. The author, borrowing from Lucan's description of Caesar and Pompeius, compares the two friends to two great oak trees, and appeals to Sir Walter Scott to celebrate the dead statesman.

> "O Scott! on that auspicious day
> That saw thy Melville's cloudless ray
> Emerge through faction's storm, thy lay
> Led out triumphal joys,
> And on his writhing foes amain
> Launched the keen arrows of disdain—
> Why lingers now thy matchless strain,
> While low thy Melville lies?"

The author describes the character of Melville in several stanzas, of which one may be quoted as a specimen.

> "Then shall consenting time revere
> Thy worth confessed—Thy judgment clear,
> Sagacious, steadfast, sound, sincere,
>   True to thy country's good;
> That shunned no toil, that duty bade,
> Courted no praise that folly paid,
> But, boastless, self-judged, undismayed,
>   Its steady path pursued."

Melville was twice married, first in 1765, and then in 1793. His first wife, a beautiful woman, was Elizabeth, daughter and heiress of David Rannie, who had bought Melville Castle, and whose money had been made in the wine trade in Leith. By his marriage with her, he is said, according to some accounts, to have obtained a hundred thousand pounds. She deserted him for another man, and a divorce followed. Her sister, Janet, married Archibald

Cockburn of Cockpen, and became the mother of Lord Cockburn.   By his first wife Melville had three daughters, and an only son, Robert Saunders Dundas, afterwards second Viscount, who himself became an eminent statesman.   The first Lord Melville married, as his second wife, Lady Jane Hope, sixth daughter of John, second Earl of Hopetoun, by whom he had no issue.   His second wife, surviving him, married in 1814 Thomas, Lord Wallace, and died in 1829.   While dealing with the family of Melville, it may be interesting to mention that Margaret, the daughter of his elder brother, the Lord President, married General John Scott of Balcomie, whose third daughter, Margaret, became the wife of George Canning, the Prime Minister.

CHAPTER XII

Melville was a man of great courage and intrepidity and never quailed before any opponent. He was strong, resolute, and determined, and was characterised by that "firm resolve," so well called by Burns "the stalk of carlehemp in man." In the strife of Parliament he never failed to stand up to those who were against him. There was a manliness in his character, said Wilberforce, which prevented him from running away from a question. He granted all the premises of his adversaries and fought them upon their own ground. Throughout his long career, in prosperous and adverse fortune, he never showed any sign of fear. "Ah! Hal Dundas," wrote Walter Scott in 1826, years after he was dead, "there was no truckling in thy day." Mrs Craigie puts into the mouth of Disraeli, whom she makes one of the characters in her charming romance, *Robert Orange*, the words, "There are many duties and difficulties in life. There is but one obligation —courage." Melville never failed to recognise the obligation of courage. In the business of politics he always believed in the bold and courageous course. He would have agreed with Cardinal Newman that to be ever safe is to be ever feeble. Horace Walpole described him as "the boldest of men." If the bold man sometimes makes mistakes, the man who makes no mistakes makes nothing. It is our business, as Burke said, rather to run the risk of falling into faults in a course which leads us to act with effect and energy than to loiter out our days without blame and without use. Amidst all his trials and difficulties Melville played the part of a strong decided resolute man. Even in his fall, when men who had courted him with servility in the days of his power turned and rent him, he neither supplicated the support of the Tories, nor bowed his head before the malignity of the Whigs. He gave a dinner at the Admiralty on the day after the Resolutions were carried against him in the House of Commons by the casting vote of the Speaker. The Duchess of Gordon was one of the guests, and said that the host received them with so much ease and cheerfulness that a stranger never could have suspected what had passed the preceding evening. He refused to lower his crest before his enemies, whatever his anxieties might be.

Melville had the advantage of possessing an appearance and manners which charmed his friends and conciliated or disarmed his opponents. He possessed in a high degree that quality of pleasing which is so valuable in public life. He was, as his nephew, Lord Cockburn said, a favourite with most men and all women. His figure was tall, manly, and advantageous. His countenance was open, cheerful, and expressive, although, in later life, it was tinged with convivial purple. He had a frank and genial bearing, which created a prejudice in his favour. He concealed, however, under that genial exterior, a shrewd and subtle mind. "The Italian maxim is a wise one," says Lord Chesterfield, "*volto schiolto e pensieri stretti*; that is, let your countenance be open, and your thoughts be close." This lesson had been grasped in its fullness by the Scottish lawyer. When he appeared to be most incautious, he was most keenly alive to his interest. In him, says

Wraxall, was exemplified the remark that *ars est celare artem*. His frank and cordial temper, his conviviality, his love of jest and good fellowship, never weakened his steady pursuit of his aims and ambitions.

The voice of Melville was strong and sonorous and enabled him to surmount the noise of a popular Assembly, and almost to command attention at moments of the greatest clamour or impatience. His speeches displayed no ornaments of style, no classic elegance, no beauties of composition. He made no pretence to scholarship or to literary gifts. He never adorned his speeches with apt citations from the writers of Greece and Rome, as Pitt and Fox did. Intent only on the matter, he never seemed to care for, or to hesitate in the choice of words, or to waste thought on the graces of elocution or delivery. But his speeches were always animated and argumentative, and never displayed any deficiency of common sense or solid ability. He never lacked lucidity or vigour, and there was always about him a certain massive and masculine force.

"He was a plain business-like speaker," says Brougham, "a man of every-day talents in the House; a clear, easy, fluent, and, from much practice, as well as strong and natural sense, a skilful debater; successful in profiting by an adversary's mistakes; distinct in opening a plan and defending a ministerial proposition; capable of producing even a great effect upon his not unwilling audiences by his broad and coarse appeals to popular prejudices, and his confident statements of facts."

Burke said that he always attended to what fell from Melville, because it had the same effect on him as if, in a camp, he heard a signal-gun, which warned him of the approach of the enemy. It is even said that Wilkes considered him the greatest orator of his time. The son and biographer of Sir John Sinclair relates that Wilkes in conversation with Sinclair declared that, while Fox had most logic, Burke most fancy, Sheridan most real wit, and Pitt excelled in command of words and ingenuity of argument, yet Melville, with all the disadvantages of being a Scotsman, was "our greatest orator." There was much sound sense, and no rubbish in his speeches, said Wilkes. One cannot help having a suspicion that Wilkes was not wholly serious in his talk with his credulous Scottish friend. To place Melville above such a galaxy as Fox, Burke, Sheridan, and Pitt, verges on the ludicrous.

The testimony of Lord Holland as to the oratorical powers of Melville is less favourable than that of Wilkes.

"His parliamentary merits consisted," says Lord Holland, "chiefly in outward appearance, spirit, and readiness; an unblushing countenance, a manly figure, a sort of grotesque hoaxing eloquence, conveyed in a loud voice and a provincial dialect, which was neither pleasantry, nor invective, and yet reminded one of both. He never hesitated in making any assertion, and without attempting to answer an argument, he either treated it as quite preposterous, or, after some bold misstatements and inapplicable maxims, confidently alleged that he had refuted it. These resources in debate, such as they were, he had always at hand."

Lord Holland quotes a statement by Fox that Melville never failed to speak with effect unless when, by some strange fatality, he happened thoroughly to understand the subject on which he spoke, and then he was long, dull, and tedious beyond all sufferance.

Melville was a determined votary of pleasure, and his gallantries and drinking bouts were favourite themes of satirists and caricaturists. In a *Political Eclogue*, entitled "Rose or the Complaint," parodied from Virgil's *Formosum pastor Corydon ardebat Alexin*, and published in 1785, the author, observing on the predilections of some distinguished persons about town, well-known for their gallantries, says,

> "What various tastes divide the fickle town,
> One likes the fair, and one admires the brown,
> The stately, Queensb'ry; Hinchinbrook, the small:
> Thurlow loves servant-maids; Dundas loves all."

Melville had brought with him from Scotland the deep-drinking habits of the nation. His love of wine he shared with Pitt, who, in spite of his austere character, was a heavy drinker. *Narratur et prisci Catonis saepe mero caluisse virtus.* Stothard, the painter, used to relate that he stayed at an inn on the Kent Road, when Pitt and Dundas put up at it for a night on their way from Walmer. He stated that he was told by the waiter next morning that they had drunk seven bottles. The lampoons and caricatures of the day frequently dwell on the bibulous tendencies of Pitt and Melville. A characteristic print by Gillray in 1795 represents one of the jovial scenes at the country house of Dundas at Wimbledon, with both statesmen in a condition of intoxication. Pitt is attempting to fill his glass from the wrong end of the bottle, while his companion, Melville, grasping pipe and bumper, ejaculates, "Billy, my boy—all my joy!" In the mock journal annexed to the *Criticisms on the Rolliad*, Melville is represented in one place as repentant after a bout. There is an entry in 1788, "Came home in a very melancholy mood—returned thanks in a short prayer for our narrow escape—drank a glass of brandy—confessed my sins—determined to reform, and sent to Wilberforce for a good book—a very worthy and religious young man that—like him much—always votes with us."

Neither Pitt nor Melville, however, allowed his

proclivity for wine to interfere with business except on one or two well-known occasions. Lord Sidmouth records that he never knew Pitt to take too much wine, if he had anything to do, except upon one occasion. Pitt had left the House of Commons with Melville in the hour between two election ballots, in order to dine. When he returned, he was unexpectedly called up to answer a personal attack made upon him by William Lambton, the father of the first Lord Durham. When he spoke, it was evident to his friends that he had taken too much wine. Next morning Mr Ley, the Clerk Assistant of the House of Commons, told the Speaker that he had felt quite ill ever since Pitt's exhibition on the previous evening. It gave him, he said, a violent headache. When this was repeated to Pitt, he remarked that he thought that was an excellent arrangement—that he should have the wine, and the Clerk the headache. The episode became the subject of endless jest and wit. One epigram, in which Pitt is supposed to address Melville, is well known,

> "I cannot see the Speaker, Hal; can you?"
> "Not see the Speaker? hang it, I see two!"

Wraxall records another occasion in 1784, on which the two statesmen gave evidence of unusual elevation. Returning very late one night on horseback to Wimbledon, from Addiscombe, the seat of Mr Jenkinson, near Croydon, where the party had dined, Thurlow, Pitt, and Melville found the turnpike-gate situated between Tooting and Streatham thrown open. Being, as Wraxall says, elevated above their usual prudence, and having no servant near them, they passed through the gate at a brisk pace, without stopping to pay the toll, regardless of the remonstrances and threats of the turnpike-keeper. Indignant at being cheated, the keeper ran after them, and, believing them to be highwaymen who had recently committed some depredations in the neighbourhood, he discharged the contents of his blunderbuss at their backs, but happily without injury.

Melville was, as the reader must have already realised, very tenacious of office—a characteristic often thrown in his teeth. His opponents constantly charged him with brazen-faced pursuit of his individual interests. Among the political miscellanies appended to the *Criticisms on the Rolliad* is a parody of the witches' incantation in *Macbeth*, and among the ingredients thrown into the cauldron are named,

> "Clippings of Corinthian brass
> From the visage of Dundas."

It must be admitted that there was something of the political Dugald Dalgetty in Melville. Like all "men of business" in politics, he liked to be in power and was ready to suit himself to circumstances. As Lord Lytton said, he grafted his talents on the healthiest fruit trees, and trained them with due care on the sunny side of the wall,

> "Office was made for him, and he for it;
> He felt that truth, and glued his soul to Pitt.
> No shrewder minister e'er served a throne,
> Or join'd his country's interests with his own."

When Shelburne saw that the days of his administration were numbered, it is said that he sent for Melville, and told him the story of the Jacobite Duke of Perth. The Duke, said Shelburne, had a country neighbour and friend, who came to him one morning with the white cockade of the Jacobites in his hat. "What is the meaning of this?" asked the Duke. "I wish to show your Grace," replied his friend, "that I am resolved to follow your fortunes."

The Duke snatched the hat from his head, took the cockade out of it, and threw it into the fire, saying, "My situation and duty compel me to take this line, but that is no reason why you should ruin yourself and your family." Lord Shelburne went on to say that it would be necessary for him to retire from office, but that he wished Melville to have early notice of his intention, so that he might be prepared for what must happen. One of the best lampoons on Melville's easy principles is the passage in the *Criticisms on the Rolliad*, in which he is described as one,

> "Whose exalted soul
> No bonds of vulgar prejudice control.
> Of shame unconscious in his bold career,
> He spurns that honour which the weak revere,
> For, true to public virtue's patriot plan,
> He loves *the minister*, and not *the man*,
> Alike the advocate of North and wit,
> The friend of Shelburne and the guide of Pitt.
> His ready tongue with sophistries at will,
> Can say, unsay, and be consistent still;
> This day can censure, and the next retract,
> In speech extol, and stigmatize in act;
> Turn and re-turn; whole hours at Hastings bawl,
> Defend, praise, thank, affront him, and recall.
> By opposition, he his king shall court;
> And damn the People's cause by his support."

In 1792 Mr Courtenay twitted Melville in the House of Commons with offering his services on every change of administration, by calling out "Wha wants me?" The phrase gave rise to a ballad entitled, "Wha wants me?" which was sung for months in the streets of Edinburgh to the tune of *My daddy is a canker'd carle*. Melville himself was frequently serenaded with it while in the Scottish capital, but as he always regarded gibes at his

inconsistency with indifference, if not amusement, the
singers grew tired of troubling him. Another ballad with
the same title as the last, sung to the tune of *He's low
down, he's in the broom*, is in the British Museum Library.
One verse runs,

> "Dear Pitt! is it not hard indeed,
> Such wicked jibes should pass,
> Against the pure and patriot creed
> Of thy belov'd Dundas?
> But let them praise, or let them blame,
> I care not a bawbee;
> My text shall ever be the same—
> 'Sirs, wha wants me?'
> Wha wants me, my friends?
> Wha wants me?
> My text shall ever be the same—
> 'Sirs, wha wants me?'"

Melville was a steady and determined friend, who, as
Brougham said, only stood the faster by those who wanted
him the more. He would not give up his adherents even
in their errors or their faults. His loyalty to Trotter has
been already referred to. There was something in him of
the spirit of the Highlander, who, when he heard a person
declare that he would stand by his friend, when he was in
the right, expressed his indignation at this half-hearted
declaration, and proclaimed his resolve to stand by a
friend at all times, right or wrong. He was totally void
of all affectation, all pride, all pretension. He never, in
the days of his greatness, ignored or forgot the friends of
his youth. In the relations of private life he was affectionate and warm-hearted. A month before his death, he
wrote to Mrs Blair, the wife of the Lord President, "If
you ask me what character gives the fairest chance for
a uniformity of good conduct and happiness through life,

I answer an affectionate and warm heart under the guidance of a sound heart and cultivated understanding." Mr Maconochie, who has examined Melville's numerous letters to Mrs Blair, says that this sentiment recurs again and again in the correspondence. In his early days, when he walked the boards of the Parliament House, his happy temper and manners, and friendly open-hearted disposition, rendered him a universal favourite among his brother advocates. In his own home at Melville, or riding about the woods of Arniston, he was simple-hearted and kindly, taking an interest in country pursuits, and fond of meeting old friends and neighbours. He was greatly loved by children and by old ladies. Lord Cockburn speaks warmly of his kindness and playfulness with children, and both Cockburn and Lockhart describe his habit, when revisiting Edinburgh in the days of his greatness, of assiduously calling on the old ladies, with whom he had been acquainted in the days of his youth. He might be seen going about, and climbing the lofty staircases of the Old Town closes, to pay his respects to ancient widows and maidens, who had been kind to him in his early days. It is probable, says Lockhart, that he gained more by this than he could have gained by almost any other thing, even in the good opinion of people, who might themselves be vainly desirous of having an interview with the great statesman.

The enormous correspondence of Melville, both published and unpublished, gives some idea of the vast amount of patronage, which he exercised, and of the extent to which he assisted his friends. As the years advanced, the burden on his shoulders became heavier and heavier. "A shade of melancholy pervades his letters," says Omond, "the melancholy and dissatisfaction

of a man, who is constantly brought in contact with mean
and greedy placemen, who is fast losing faith in the purity
of motive, and even the common honesty of those he has
to deal with, and who can never be sure that ulterior views
do not lurk behind the common civilities which he receives
even from his friends." Assailed as he was by never
ceasing applications, it is not surprising that, as he waxed
older, he sometimes inclined to be cynical. But he never
became hard or bitter or unsympathetic. There was no
gall in his temper. The ingratitude of those whom he
had served sometimes pained him, and he could not help
occasionally giving utterance to his grief. "Had I remained at the Scotch Bar," he said on one occasion,
"I must soon have reached one of the highest judicial
offices in Scotland, and might have spent a life of comfort
and independence. In the important capacity of a judge,
I might have been of use to my native country; whereas
by entering on the career of politics, I have been exposed
to much obloquy, and have latterly experienced the
basest ingratitude." But that ingratitude, although on
more than one occasion he felt it keenly, did not sour his
kindly nature.

"He's truly valiant, that can wisely suffer
  The worst that man can breathe; and make his wrongs
  His outsides; wear them like his raiment carelessly;
  And ne'er prefer his injuries to his heart
  To bring it into danger."

Melville was truly valiant in the spirit of Shakespere's
lines. He was too strong a man to indulge in unavailing
regrets or to brood over past injuries. Like old James
Carlyle of Ecclefechan, he "never looked back." "I hate
to indulge retrospective melancholy," he wrote once to
Grenville. "As I cannot cure what is past by repining

at it, I shall be silent," he wrote to Admiral Young in 1804, with reference to something that had displeased him.   He did not allow his spirit to be clouded by misfortunes or blunders.   He did not repine at the inevitable; he accepted it with composure, and went on with his work. Lord Holland, in his venomous critique of Melville already quoted, says that no man was more implacable in his hatreds.   Nothing could be more untrue.   He did not allow even the persecution, which threw a shadow over the evening of his days, to sour or spoil him.   An incident recorded by Wilberforce, who had supported the hostile action of Whitbread, may be cited in proof of this assertion.

"We did not meet for a long time," says Wilberforce, "and all his connections most violently abused me.   About a year before he died, we met in the stone passage which leads from the Horse Guards to the Treasury.   We came suddenly upon each other, just in the open part, where the light struck upon our faces.   We saw one another, and at first I thought he was passing on, but he stopped and called out, 'Ah, Wilberforce, how do you do?' and gave me a hearty shake by the hand. I would have given a thousand pounds for that shake.   I never saw him afterwards."

CHAPTER XIII

Melville was honoured from time to time by the Universities of his native land. He received the degree of Doctor of Laws in 1789 from his alma mater, the University of Edinburgh. He filled the post of Lord Rector of the University of Glasgow from 1781 to 1783. He was appointed Chancellor of the University of St Andrews in 1788. Unlike Pitt, he was ready to help artists and men of letters, more especially those who were his countrymen. Pitt was singularly indifferent to the claims of literature, perhaps because he was pressed by more urgent demands. When it was proposed to him in 1794 that the Government should buy the anatomical collections of John Hunter, the eminent surgeon, Pitt replied, "What! buy preparations! Why, I have not money enough to purchase gunpowder!" Melville exhibited a more sympathetic attitude towards the literati of his time and country than Pitt did, and was not averse to playing the part of a Scottish Maecenas. It is to the credit of the Scottish statesman that he appreciated and honoured his great countryman, Adam Smith. It was at a dinner at the house of Dundas in Wimbledon that Pitt paid Adam Smith the compliment that has been so often quoted. The philosopher was one of the last to arrive, and, when he entered, all rose to their feet. "Be seated, gentlemen," said Smith. "No," replied Pitt, "we will stand till you are first seated, for we are all your scholars." Dundas was present at the dinner at Pitt's house, when Adam Smith paid an equally high compliment to Pitt. "What an extraordinary man Pitt is," said Adam Smith, "he understands my ideas better than I do myself[1]."

Alexander Carlyle of Inveresk recommended both Archibald Alison and Adam Ferguson to the good offices of Dundas. In one and the same letter he is found thanking Dundas for taking "Archy" by the hand, and urging him to help Ferguson, to whose work on *The Roman Republic* the world had, in Carlyle's opinion, done gross injustice. "I was always in hopes that some of you would have quoted it in the House of Commons, as Charles Fox did Principal Watson's *Philip*, for some of his purposes in the time of the American War...but I have been disappointed." Dr Sommerville of Jedburgh says that, when he was collecting materials for his historical work, Melville interested himself in his pursuits with great frankness and zeal, and further showed his appreciation of Sommerville's merits by getting him appointed to a chaplaincy at £50 a year. Sommerville says that, at a Royal levée in 1800, Melville introduced him to Pitt, who had done for him what Carlyle wanted Melville to do for Ferguson. When doleful prophecies as to the effect of the union between Great Britain and Ireland had been made in the House of Commons, Pitt had quoted Sommerville's *History of Queen Anne*, to show the change of sentiment that had taken place in Scotland after a few years' experience of the happy effects of the union between England and Scotland.

[1] Another version of the anecdote is given in Pellew's *Life of Sidmouth*, I, 151.

Melville had the privilege of enjoying the friendship and homage of Sir Walter Scott. Scott always professed to believe in his disinterestedness, and, after his death, was always ready to do his memory justice. Melville was a frequent visitor to the poet's house in Castle Street, Edinburgh, and a great favourite in the happy circle there. He entered with such simple-heartedness into all the ways of the family circle that it had come to be an established rule for the children "to sit up to supper" when Melville dined there. In 1810 there was still talk of Melville going out to India as Governor-General, and Scott wrote to his brother that, if this actually happened, and Melville were willing to take him in a good situation, he would not hesitate "to pitch the Court of Session and the booksellers to the devil," and try his fortune in another climate.

It was the good fortune of Melville to be able to assist in relieving the *res angustae domi* of the most interesting Scot of his time, if one might apply that word to the last Prince of the House of Stuart. At the end of the eighteenth century all the glory and romance of the ancient Scottish dynasty was centred in an aged Cardinal living in poverty on the slopes of Frascati. The line of Robert Bruce, and James the Poet, and James of the Fiery Face, and James of the Iron Belt, and Mary, and Charles the Martyr, had ended in an old priest celebrating the Mass and dreaming of the glories of his ancestors in an Italian palace. In 1799 Cardinal Stefano Borgia, a member of the Italian branch of the great Spanish House of Borgia, wrote to his friend, Sir John Hippesley, urging the claims of the poverty-stricken Cardinal Henry Stuart to the consideration of the British government. Hippesley, who had married a daughter of Sir John Stuart of Allanbank, and was thus connected by marriage with the royal clan of Scotland, at once communicated with Andrew Stuart of Castlemilk, the author of the *Genealogical History of the Royal Stewarts*, who is now best known for the active part he took in the Douglas Cause. Andrew Stuart, who was acquainted with Cardinal Henry, and who was also a friend of Melville, presented a formal memorial to the latter. Melville in his turn communicated with Pitt, who approached the King, and showed him the letter of Hippesley and the memorial of Andrew Stuart. As a result of the movement an annuity was settled upon the Cardinal, and his closing years were relieved from the fear of penury and distress. If the words of Churchill, the poet, were true, that the Scots of the eighteenth century,

> "Howe'er they wear the mask of art,
> Still love a Stuart in their heart,"

it must have afforded Melville very real satisfaction to assist in providing for the old age of the last Prince of the line that his ancestors had served.

Melville was frequently criticised, as has been already stated, for his national partialities, and for his practice of favouring his own countrymen. Ever since the Union there had been sporadic outbursts against the eagerness of the Scots to come to England, and their rapid attainment of wealth and position outside their own country.

> "Now Scot and English are agreed,
> And Saunders hastes to cross the Tweed,
> Where, such the splendours that attend him,
> His very mother scarce had kend him.
> His metamorphosis behold,
> From Glasgow frieze to cloth of gold;
> His back-sword, with the iron hilt,
> To rapier, fairly hatch'd and gilt;
> Was ever seen a gallant braver!
> His very bonnet's grown a beaver."

The accession of the unpopular Bute to power in 1760 had given rise to a ferocious display of spleen and scurrility against the Scots, which left a long trail of ill-feeling behind it. It was only by slow degrees that more frequent intercourse mitigated the sentiment of national antipathy. Communications greatly increased between Bute's accession to power, and that of Pitt. In 1760 a stage coach set out from Edinburgh once a month for London, and consumed fifteen days upon the road. On the eve of Pitt's accession to power, there were fifteen coaches to London weekly, which made the journey in four days. This fact alone is extremely significant.

When Melville came to the front, the feeling towards the Scots was ceasing to be vicious, and was rather becoming one of mockery and derision. Two typical anecdotes will show the sort of gibe that delighted the Englishman at the end of the eighteenth century. Lord Eldon relates that Boswell once came to him in his chambers in Lincoln's Inn, and asked him for his definition of Taste, remarking that he had that morning got the definitions of Dundas, Sir Archibald Macdonald, and John Anstruther. "Taste, according to my definition," said Lord Eldon, after some pressure, "is the judgment which Dundas, Macdonald, Anstruther, and you manifested when you determined to quit Scotland and to come into the South." It is said that Melville did not always take those gibes as goodnaturedly as Boswell did. He was desired by George the Third to do something for a man named Bedingfield who had come to the King's rescue when his coach was assailed by a mob at the opening of Parliament in October, 1795. When Melville asked Bedingfield what could be done for him, the latter replied that the best thing that Melville could do for him was to make him a Scotchman. The minister is said to have angrily dismissed the humourist, and it was only after pressure on the part of the King that Bedingfield was rewarded by being appointed to an office.

The antipathy to the Scots lingered on even into the nineteenth century. When Melville ceased, as the result of the proceedings against him, to be First Lord of the Admiralty, William Windham mentioned, as one of the good results following from his resignation, that the Admiralty would be taken out of hands that would soon have given Great Britain a Scottish navy. As late as 1807, the old flouts, and gibes, and jeers, were still being trotted out. In July of that year Rowlandson published a caricature entitled " More Scotchmen or Johnny Maccree Opening his New Budget." Dundas in Highland garb is opening the mouth of his sack, from whence is issuing an interminable stream of Scotchmen, who are trooping steadily on the road to fortune, through the portals of St Stephen's.

Although autocrat of Scotland, Melville was not, like most autocrats, hated or even unpopular. He was too much a man of the world, as Cockburn said, not to live well with his opponents, when they would let him, and he was totally incapable of personal harshness or unkindness. No human omnipotence, said Cockburn, could have been exercised with a smaller amount of just offence. His position of absolute power did not turn his head, or make him selfish and tyrannical. "He was not merely worshipped by his many personal friends," says Cockburn, "and by the numerous idolaters, whom the idol fed; but was respected by the reasonable of his opponents; who, though doomed to suffer by his power, liked the individual; against whom they had nothing to say, except that he was not on their side, and reserved his patronage for his supporters." They knew that he had no vindictive desire to persecute or crush those who refused to be brought into his system. Cockburn, who was an ardent Whig, and hated the system, over which Melville presided, states that he was the very man for Scotland at that time, and was a Scotchman of whom his country might be proud. He states as facts which ought to mitigate censure that Melville did not make the bad elements with which he had to work, and that he did not abuse them.

Melville loved to go to Scotland, and to throw off, as far as he could, the cares and worries of office. He was greatly attached to his native country, and especially to his Highland home, Dunira, in Perthshire. He always spent as much of his time as he could among the Highland mountains. In September, 1785, for example, he writes to the Duke of Rutland, "After being almost faged (*sic*) to death, I set out for Scotland this afternoon to shoot and hunt for two months." Although a Lowlander, he had a strong sympathy with Highland feelings and traditions. He was no enemy, he wrote in 1793 to the Countess of Sutherland, but very much the reverse, to the principles and consequences of clanship. His Highland sympathies were evidenced by his Act for the restoration of the Forfeited Estates, and by his repeal of the provision forbidding the wearing of the Highland dress.

Melville liked, when in Scotland, to revive the jollity and convivial habits of an earlier time. Like Agricola, *ubi officio satisfactum, nulla ultra potestatis persona; tristitiam et adrogantiam et avaritiam exuerat.* When he had fulfilled his official duties, he no longer personated the man of power, but threw off all sternness and stiffness, and airs of state. He would sometimes revisit with friends the taverns and laigh cellars of Old Edinburgh, which he had frequented in his youthful days. Somebody once rallied Sir Walter Scott, as a young man, on the slovenliness of his clothes, and he replied, "They be good enough for drinking in. Let us go and have some oysters in the Covenant Close." To eat oysters and drink in the Covenant Close was a principal feature of the life of the young advocate in those times, and a feature on which Melville in the days of his greatness looked back with regret. Cockburn depicts Melville as taking part in a curious convivial usage that still lingered in Scotland. It was the custom of men in high position to meet in rural inns and alehouses and there, freed from the restraints that bound them in their homes, give themselves up to Bacchanalian excesses. Scott describes in *Waverley* how a party of gentlemen left the mansion-house of Tullyveolan to drink in Lucky Macleary's wretched howf in the village. Cockburn describes a similar occasion when the Duke of Buccleugh, Melville, Robert Dundas, Hepburn of Clerkington, and several others of the Midlothian gentry, left their luxurious homes to meet in a wretched alehouse at Middleton for a day of what they regarded as freedom and jollity.

"We found them," says Cockburn, "roaring and singing and laughing in a low-roofed room scarcely large enough to hold them, with wooden chairs and a⁻sanded floor....There was plenty of wine, particularly claret, in rapid circulation on the table; but my eye was chiefly attracted by a huge bowl of hot whisky punch, the steam of which was almost dropping from the roof, while the odour was enough to perfume the whole parish....How they did joke and laugh! with songs, and toasts, and disputation, and no want of practical fun."

With all his social and convivial qualities, Melville was pre-eminently a man of business. He possessed a great capacity for the transaction of affairs, and, in particular, what Pitt described as a "turn for facilitating business." He had no shining parts; he did not possess, for example, the intellectual gifts that make a great war minister, but he had the qualities of a capable man of affairs. He was successful, like Poppaeus Sabinus, *nullam ob eximiam artem, sed quod par negotiis neque supra erat*. He was equal to the conduct of affairs, and not above it. He was possessed of a restless industry and untiring application. He showed a prompt comprehension of information communicated to him, and a ready capacity for improving it, and applying it to existing circumstances. His training at the Scottish Bar had disciplined his mind to the drudgery of the desk, and helped him to systematise as well as to direct the machinery of administration. Wilberforce wrote in his journal in January, 1792, of a visit to Pitt at Wimbledon. "A long discussion with Dundas after dinner," he says, "a most excellent man of business...his diligence shames me." Like Catiline, Melville *maximum bonum in celeritate putabat*. He attached great importance to celerity in the conduct of business. Lord Holland, in the ill-natured critique of Melville, that has been more than once referred to, says that his talents for business consisted rather in despatch than in great penetration or judgment, and that, if his business was not always highly finished, it was soon got out of hand He goes on to quote Windham's gibe that Melville performed coarse jobs well, but that he was quite unfit for cabinet work. One may readily agree with Holland's comment that Windham himself was perhaps an illustration that despatch in business and readiness of decision are qualities not less essential in a minister than acuteness of understanding and firmness of mind.

In the various departments, which Melville controlled,

he left permanent monuments of his wisdom and energy.
His services to the Indian Empire were enormous. He
applied himself to the management of Indian affairs with
intense application, and exhibited great foresight in providing for the extension of territory and the development
of British interests. He selected the ablest rulers of our
Eastern dominions, and may be said to have consolidated
the mighty empire, which Warren Hastings had preserved.
It was in his office of minister for India that his great
capacity for affairs shone chiefly forth, and that he gave
solid and long-continued proof of an indefatigable industry,
which neither the distractions of debate in Parliament, nor
the convivial habits of the man, ever could interrupt or
relax. "His celebrated reports," says Brougham, "upon
all the complicated questions of our Asiatic policy, although
they may not stand a comparison with some of Mr Burke's
in the profundity and enlargement of general views, any
more than their style can be compared with his, are never-
theless performances of the greatest merit, and repositories
of information upon that vast subject, unrivalled for clear-
ness and extent." It is true that James Mill in his history
of British India—"a solemn slander in several volumes
upon British rule in India," as it has been called—belittles
the work of Melville in connexion with the East. He says
that the mind of Melville was active and meddling, and
that he was careful to exhibit the appearance of a great
share in the government of India, but that any advice,
which he ever gave, for the government of India, was
either very obvious or wrong. Such a criticism as that
is the unworthy production of political prejudice, and is
wholly undeserving of the slightest credence.

Dundas was ahead of his times in his views about
India, as about many other matters. He foresaw the

possibility of an attack upon the British dominions in the East through Persia, or some part of Asia, and it was upon this ground that he insisted with the East India Company on establishing a resident at Bagdad. In 1783 he advocated the appointment of a Secretary of State for India, an office which was not created till 1858. Melville was also keenly alive to the importance of Egypt. In April, 1798, he wrote to Lord Spencer saying that, but for the demands of the navy and the want of military force, he would long before have drawn the attention of Government to the importance of getting possession of Egypt. If any great European power should ever get possession of that country, he wrote, the keeping of it would cost nothing, and the nation so getting possession of Egypt would in his opinion, he said, be possessed of the master key to all the commerce of the world. Melville was greatly distressed when Napoleon established himself on the Nile, and wrote to Lord Spencer that no price was too dear to pay for getting the French out of Egypt. "The circumstance," he said, "haunts me night and day."

As Treasurer of the Navy, and First Lord of the Admiralty, he rendered great and important services to the navy. As Admiral Byam Martin, whose journals and letters have been published by the Navy Records Society, says, no minister was ever placed at the helm of naval affairs, who did more for the advantage of the service and the immediate interests of the seamen than Melville. One of the great evils of his time was the custom of impressing seamen for enlistment in the navy. Melville was very anxious to put an end to this system. He clung, said Martin, with great perseverance, to the hope of being able to abolish impressment. But he found it utterly impossible to effect this reform in the circumstances of his time. He introduced various regulations into the naval service, which secured for him the appellation of the "seaman's friend." Whitbread in his speech at the Impeachment admitted that the widows and orphans of the sailors had been the objects of his peculiar care. The fraudulent custom of forging the wills of seamen, which was frequently practised by unscrupulous sharpers, was stopped, and provisions were made for the families of those employed in the navy, when the breadwinners were absent.

While it is true that Melville used his great patronage to strengthen his own position and the administration to which he belonged, there is plenty of evidence that he did not allow personal preferences or the desire to assist his friends to blind him to the interests of the State. The level of character and ability among the young Scotsmen, to whom so much of his patronage went, was so high that no evil consequences resulted from his confidence in them. Although he was surrounded by wirepullers and expectant placemen, he was never unduly influenced by them. Mixing with all classes, he formed his own opinions from what he heard and saw. Lord Holland states that he was a steady and unscrupulous promoter of the interests of his followers, and that in furthering the views of his friends, or thwarting those of his opponents, he was quite regardless of the interests of the country. This statement is the mere outcome of party venom. There is abundant testimony that it is not true. Wilberforce says that he was with him and Pitt, when they looked through "the Red Book," to see who was the most proper person to send as Governor-General to India. "It should be mentioned to Dundas's honour," says Wilberforce, "that, having the disposal of the most important office in the

King's gift, he did not make it a means of gaining favour with any great family, or of obliging any of his country-men, but appointed the fittest person he could find (Sir John Shore). Three several times have I stated this fact in the House of Commons, and never once has it been mentioned in any of the papers." Again Wilberforce says in his diary under 17th March, 1801, "Dundas well deserves his pension, though at first honestly refused it. The King recommended a nobleman for office—Dundas refused, saying 'none but who (are) fit could be placed in those offices'; and now trying hard to persuade Charles Grant to go to India. Highly disinterested." Even in the case of his relations he would not do that which was detrimental to the public service. In March, 1784, he is found recommending his nephew, Captain Charles Ross of the Third Dragoons, for promotion, to the Duke of Rutland, Lord Lieutenant of Ireland. In December, 1786, however, he wrote again saying that it had been rumoured that the promotion of his nephew would be displeasing to an officer of merit in another corps, and asking Rutland not to proceed in the matter.

It is impossible to claim for Melville a position in politics like that of Pitt or Fox. He represented no political principle, and founded no party. If he had any exemplar in politics at all, it was Chatham, whom he greatly admired and to whom, as he once said in the House of Commons, he had been taught to look up with reverence from his earliest youth. Melville was not made of the stuff out of which great political leaders are formed, but was rather of the type of strong and reliable henchmen. He lives in history only as a statesman of masculine vigour and indomitable courage who was devoted to his country. He was guided, not by comprehensive theories, but by the everyday requirements of Party warfare. Cicero in more than one of his speeches lays down that a statesman should regulate his conduct, like a ship, by the condition of the political weather. He should not fight out political enmities to the end, but should have regard to the general good. He should not always defend the same opinions, but rather those which the position of the State, the bias of the times, and the interests of peace may require. If Melville had been familiar with the works of Cicero, as Pitt was, he would no doubt have endorsed this view.

Mr Fortescue, in some interesting comments on the character of Melville, stamps him as "commonplace." He points out that his peculiar gifts, his shrewd perception of the political tendencies of the moment, his cunning divination as to whether it would be most profitable to oppose or follow or lead them, were the supreme expression of the commonplace. It implied intimate sympathy with the commonplace mind, intimate knowledge of all commonplace natures, boundless command of commonplace ability, boundless wealth in commonplace resources. This is to a large extent true, and, if Melville had not had this power of sympathising with the commonplace, he could not have done for Pitt what he did. Pitt had to be kept in power. Without a solid parliamentary following Pitt's high ideals and lofty projects would have been futile and ineffectual. Melville had to do the work that was necessary to secure and retain Pitt's majority. He had to keep an eye on the next division, the next gazette, the next election. If his influence in Parliament was great, it was largely due to his knowledge of the commonplace mind. "The House of Commons," said Hazlitt, "hates everything but a commonplace." Sir William Fraser says that one reason of Palmerston's success was that he rarely, if ever, emerged

from commonplace and conventionality, and that he never
fired over the heads of his audience.   He states of Disraeli,
that there was nothing that Disraeli hated more than
commonplace, and there was nothing that he made more
use of.   Towards the end of his career, says Fraser, no
one appeared to win his favour, except those possessing
this.   Brilliant himself, he felt deeply that to shine was
not to succeed.   And so Melville, master of the commonplace, was a success in the House of Commons, and for
long one of its most outstanding figures.

LIST OF THE PRINCIPAL AUTHORITIES
USED BY THE AUTHOR

Stanhope's Life of Pitt, 1861-2.
Mill's History of British India, 1826.
Brougham's Sketches of Statesmen in the Reign of George III, 1871.
Jesse's Memoirs of George III, 1867.
Cockburn's Life of Jeffrey, 1852.
Lockhart's Life of Scott.
Boswell's Life of Johnson.
Walpole's Memoirs of George III, 1845.
Russell's Life and Times of Fox, 1859-66.
Life and Times of Lord Brougham, 1871.
The Rolliad, 1795.
Rosebery's Pitt, 1891.
Wright's Caricature History of the Georges (1868).
Cockburn's Memorials of His Time, 1856.
Rae's Sheridan, 1896.
Alexander Carlyle's Autobiography, 1860.
Cockburn's Journal, 1874.
Albemarle's Memoirs of Lord Rockingham, 1852.
Omond's Lord Advocates of Scotland, 1883.
The Cornwallis Correspondence, 1859.
Memoirs and Correspondence of Lord Castlereagh, 1849.
Adams' Political State of Scotland, 1887.
Yonge's Life of Lord Liverpool, 1868.
Lecky's History of England, 1892.
Diary and Correspondence of George Rose, 1860.
Life of Lord Campbell, 1881.
Letters of Lord Barham (Navy Records Society), 1896-1910.
South Africa a Century Ago, by Lady Anne Barnard, edited by W. H. Wilkins, 1901.
Diary and Correspondence of Lord Colchester, 1861.
Life of William Wilberforce, by his Sons, 1838.
Journal and Correspondence of Lord Auckland, 1861-2.
Omond's Arniston Memoirs, 1887.
Rae's Life of Adam Smith, 1895.
William Pitt and National Revival, by Holland Rose, 1911.
William Pitt and the Great War, by Holland Rose, 1911.
Pellew's Life of Lord Sidmouth, 1847.

Campbell's Lives of the Chancellors, 1845–69.
Letters of Sir James Bland Burges, edited by Hutton, 1885.
Speeches of Fox, 1815.
Wraxall's Historical Memoirs of My Own Time, 1836.
Wraxall's Posthumous Memoirs, 1836.
Memoirs of Horner, 1853.
Memoirs of Sir John Sinclair, 1837.
Works of Gillray, edited by Wright (1873).
Works of Gillray, published by Bohn (1851).
Grego's Rowlandson the Caricaturist, 1880.
Lord Holland's Memoirs of the Whig Party, 1852.
Mathieson's Awakening of Scotland, 1910.
Meikle's Scotland and the French Revolution, 1912.
Kay's Original Portraits, 1842.
The Melviad, by I-Spy-I, 3rd edition, 1805.
Life of Sir Gilbert Elliot, by Countess of Minto, 1874.
Monody on the Death of Lord Melville and Lord President
  Blair, 1811.
Grant Robertson's England under the Hanoverians, 1911.
Fortescue's History of the British Army, vol. IV, 1906.
Blackwood's Magazine, September, 1913 (article on "A Great
  Judge" by Maconochie).
Memoirs of Sir James Mackintosh, 1836.
Peter's Letters to His Kinsfolk, by Lockhart, 1819.
Memoirs of Samuel Romilly, 1840.
Craik's Century of Scottish History, 1901.
Spencer Papers (Navy Records Society), vol. I, 1913, vol. II,
  1914.
Wyndham Papers, 1913.
Fortescue's British Statesmen of the Great War, 1911.
Fitzmaurice's Life of Shelburne, 1912.
Political History of England, vols. X and XI.
Cambridge Modern History, vol. VI.
Dictionary of National Biography.
Reports of Historical MSS Commission:
  Stopford Sackville MSS, vol. I, 1904.
  MSS of J. B. Fortescue, vols. I–VIII, 1892–1912.
  MSS in Various Collections, vol. VI, 1909.
  MSS of Duke of Rutland, vol. III, 1894.
  Volume 10, Part 2 (1885).
  Thirteenth Report, Appen., 4, 6, 7 (1892–3).
Pamphlets and tracts relating to Lord Melville in the British
  Museum Library.

INDEX

For EU product safety concerns, contact us at Calle de José Abascal, 56–1°,
28003 Madrid, Spain or eugpsr@cambridge.org.

www.ingramcontent.com/pod-product-compliance
Ingram Content Group UK Ltd.
Pitfield, Milton Keynes, MK11 3LW, UK
UKHW012332130625
459647UK00009B/236